Kim,
Thank you for
coming today.
God bless your
homeschooling experience.
Love,
Silvia Escobar
Ps. 90:12

Homeschooling: Do It Afraid

Silvia Escobar

WESTBOW PRESS
A DIVISION OF THOMAS NELSON
& ZONDERVAN

Copyright © 2017 Silvia Escobar.

All rights reserved. No part of this book may be used or reproduced by any means, graphic, electronic, or mechanical, including photocopying, recording, taping or by any information storage retrieval system without the written permission of the author except in the case of brief quotations embodied in critical articles and reviews.

Scripture quotations marked (NIV) are taken from the Holy Bible, New International Version®, NIV®. Copyright © 1973, 1978, 1984, 2011 by Biblica, Inc.™ Used by permission of Zondervan. All rights reserved worldwide.

Scripture quotations are taken from the Holy Bible, New Living Translation, copyright ©1996, 2004, 2007, 2013, 2015 by Tyndale House Foundation. Used by permission of Tyndale House Publishers, Inc., Carol Stream, Illinois 60188. All rights reserved.

WestBow Press books may be ordered through booksellers or by contacting:

WestBow Press
A Division of Thomas Nelson & Zondervan
1663 Liberty Drive
Bloomington, IN 47403
www.westbowpress.com
1 (866) 928-1240

Because of the dynamic nature of the Internet, any web addresses or links contained in this book may have changed since publication and may no longer be valid. The views expressed in this work are solely those of the author and do not necessarily reflect the views of the publisher, and the publisher hereby disclaims any responsibility for them.

Any people depicted in stock imagery provided by Thinkstock are models, and such images are being used for illustrative purposes only.
Certain stock imagery © Thinkstock.

ISBN: 978-1-9736-0491-4 (sc)
ISBN: 978-1-9736-0492-1 (hc)
ISBN: 978-1-9736-0490-7 (e)

Library of Congress Control Number: 2017915717

Print information available on the last page.

WestBow Press rev. date: 11/14/2017

This book is dedicated to the God who gives me the life I never knew I wanted, the family He uses to get me there, and the friends who encouraged me to put it down on paper.

Contents

A Word About Fear ix

Chapter 1   What if We Can't Afford for Me to Stay Home? 1

Chapter 2   What if We Can't Do Everything? 15

Chapter 3   What if We Make a Mistake? 27

Chapter 4   What if My Husband and I Can't Agree? 41

Chapter 5   What About Structure vs. Freedom? 59

Chapter 6   What Will People Think? 71

Chapter 7   What if I Can't Do This? 87

Chapter 8   What if We Ruin Our Kids? 97

Chapter 9   What Will I Do When the Kids Leave? 107

Conclusion 117

A Word About Fear

When I think about fear, my mind goes back to the year when I had to confront many of my fears at once. Fears such as uncertainty, the unknown, phobias I had forgotten I had and the fear of death. My, then, fourteen year old daughter and I had decided to go on a mission's trip with four other moms and their children to Haiti. My daughter had never been on a plane, and I hadn't been outside the country for over twenty years. We committed to going before knowing how we would raise the money. We just felt that this was an answer to prayer. My daughter wanted to be a missionary and this was an opportunity for both of us to go together. It was a crazy time for it however. Any reasonable person would have said no to that opportunity. In fact, I had friends telling me to let someone else take our place or to even send my daughter with someone else. We were moving and were struggling to find the right place that would accommodate my dad who couldn't climb stairs anymore and had cancer. Our deadline to move was two months before we were going on our trip. A few weeks before we left, my dad had emergency surgery while we were still fundraising for the trip. Also, I had gone back to school that year. There was a lot of running around and a high level of anxiety, but we managed to get my dad into a physical therapy facility, we were able to fundraise all the money for the trip, we moved into a house that had more than we needed and my classes finished two days before we left!

With so many things to do before we left, I didn't really get to catch my breath until we were on the plane. Even then, it seemed like a dream. My daughter was so excited, it was contagious. When we got to Port au Prince, Haiti, we were driven to a compound that we were not allowed to leave. We were told that Port au Prince was not a safe place. For safety reasons, there were guards in front of the compound that housed missionaries. Once inside, we got our room assignment. The next day we would fly in a small MAF plane into the mountains to Pignon, our destination. The kids were excited to be there and they were talking and laughing as they got ready for bed. Meanwhile, in the bathroom I looked in the mirror and was suddenly overwhelmed with fear and anxiety. "Whose idea was this? Why am I here? What am I doing here?"

If I could have gotten off that island right then and there, I would have. But of course, I couldn't. I was stuck. I was powerless. I couldn't breathe. I paced in the bathroom trying to stop the tears, trying to stop the panic I felt, trying to stop the fear that was threatening to take complete control over me. I could hear my daughter laughing in the bedroom with her friends. "That's because she doesn't know the dangers that lurk in a place like this," I thought. Still, I didn't want to ruin this trip for her. I had to get out of the bathroom and show her I was just as excited as she was. Or at least not show the fear I was feeling. When I finally did get out of the bathroom, I sat on the bed (all the while wondering if there were any bugs under it or under the covers). As everyone around me talked and laughed, I wrote in my journal the following entry:

> Well, I think I'm crazy. We are in Haiti. I can't believe I'm doing this! Whose idea was this? I am just about going out of my comfort zone in every way imaginable. I am confronting just about every fear I have! Who does that! We're supposed to do them

one at a time! I'm afraid of heights and I'm going on a MAF plane tomorrow. I hate going on a plane without my family and I left them at home for a week. I need to know what's going on at home and I can't communicate with anyone. I hate total darkness and I'm going to a town where the generator goes off at night. I can't stand bugs and spiders and there's a dead tarantula on the road and a roach in the bathroom. What was I thinking? If I could, I would pack up and leave right now!

Of course, I can't. I feel like I'm about to burst! I could cry for hours just thinking of how I'm going to survive these next few days. But I can't go there. I can't think ahead. I've got to take it one step at a time.

I'm putting my faith in You, Lord. I pray you give me the courage, the peace and the focus to let myself go and concentrate on what I'm here for. I am so absorbed by my fears, that I can't breadth! I can't vent them. I'll ruin it for everyone.

'I will lay down and sleep in peace. For you alone, oh Lord, make me dwell in safety.'

Make this verse real to me, Lord. I pray, I beg, I believe, in Jesus' name, amen.

What happened next was a miracle! From the top of my head to the bottom of my feet, I began to feel a peace, a calmness. It's funny that even though I had just asked for it, now that I was feeling it, I was wondering what was going on. I didn't understand it. And then it hit me—the peace that surpasses all understanding! I was experiencing it right then and there! From that moment on, I enjoyed the week. I loved the MAF plane. I even took pictures! During the whole trip I was at peace, but I was aware that it was God who had given me that peace. I was also aware there was a closed door in my mind. If I opened it, the fear would come back. If I started to entertain the thoughts that brought me fear, I would be in danger of panicking again, o I deliberately stayed away from that door and concentrated on the moment. As long as I trusted God I would be fine. And I was. My mission's trip to Haiti was a life changing experience for me on so many levels—especially regarding my understanding of fear.

As moms we are so often motivated by fear; as homeschool moms even more so. We have taken on so much responsibility for our children's future that we can't help but worry and be afraid. I can see it in my life, as I'm sure you can see it in yours. Like in my trip to Haiti, I have often wondered, "Whose idea was this?" I have moments of doubt, of anger, of disappointment. I have had moments when I've thought, "I change my mind. I don't want to do this after all." But from where I stand now, having finished homeschooling four, still homeschooling two more and being a grandmother, I can say that I have experienced peace. I am enjoying the journey. But like on my Haiti trip, I am aware of a closed door of fear in my mind. At any given time, no matter how much I have witnessed God's faithfulness, no matter how much I've trusted Him before, if I open that door of fear, the fears will come back. The difference now is that the more I see God's faithfulness, the less likely I am to open that door. It doesn't tempt me as much as it used to, though it will never completely go away. I just have to do it afraid.

It is my desire to share with you my own struggle with fear and how that has impacted my decisions, but also how God has been faithful and shown me how to do it afraid. It is a lifelong process, but the less we are motivated by fear, the freer we become to make decisions; to enjoy our families; to appreciate the process of homeschooling; to see the hand of God even in those things that seemingly go awry.

Chapter 1

What if We Can't Afford for Me to Stay Home?

Homeschooling: Do it on a Tight Budget
(The Fear of Scarcity)

When we decided to homeschool, we did it as a step of faith. I had become a stay-at-home mom a few years before, and I was pregnant with our third child, Isaac. We pulled our oldest son, Alex, out of the private school he was attending at the end of third grade, and our second son, Miguel, was going into kindergarten. As time went on, we did well financially. My husband worked in real estate and it was a good season for him. In 2000, looking for a bigger home, we moved out of the city and bought a house in the northwest suburbs of Chicago. By this time, we had been homeschooling for seven years and had five children: Alex, Miguel, Isaac, Christy, and David. We knew no other homeschoolers because there weren't any where we lived in Chicago, but when we moved to the suburbs, we suddenly found ourselves in a neighborhood with four other homeschool families! We joined the support group and fell in love with our homeschool community. We went on the field trips, joined homeschool gym classes, paid for piano lessons, and bought all kinds of books for homeschoolers. We were having fun,

Silvia Escobar

enjoying all these opportunities. We had another child, Kathy, in 2002, making it a grand total of six. For a few years we were very comfortable. We paid our mortgage, our two vehicles, our health insurance, our bills and made payments on our oldest son's college tuition. We had some debt, but it was manageable. We didn't have to face fears of uncertainty. Then my husband got sick. In less than six months, everything changed.

At first, we thought he had the flu, but soon it was obvious that it was much more serious. For months we went to doctors and did tests to find out what was wrong. My husband was dying, and we didn't know from what. We found out our insurance didn't cover everything. I found out I was expecting twins. Three months into my pregnancy, I had a miscarriage, which added more medical bills. Two months later, Arturo was taken in for surgery. The next day, my mom was taken to the emergency room in Chicago. Thirty days later, my mom passed away. Those days were filled with anxiety, fear, lack of resources, and hospital visits. In the midst of all that uncertainty, there was homeschooling that couldn't get done while I was gone. During all of this, our income was spiraling down to poverty level. In a matter of months, we were in financial uncertainty.

Many of you can relate, although the circumstances that brought you to financial uncertainty might be different. Someone once said, "Crises come to us all. If you haven't gone through one, it's because you're in the middle of one. And if you're not in the middle of one, get ready, because it's coming." One of the biggest risks that I see when we go through crises is the pressure we feel to stop homeschooling. Our tendency as human beings is to give way to fear when we see changes that are affecting or might affect our family. Fears that are founded on real possibilities. Losing jobs. Losing our savings. Not being able to save for our kids' college education. Losing our house.

Regardless of the kinds of fears we have, fear can lead us to make bad decisions. Fear is a poor master. As our nation suffers the consequences of an unprecedented national debt, as we are affected by the chaos around us, what will be our response as Christian women, wives, mothers, homeschoolers and homemakers? What things will change? What things have already changed? How will we respond in times of desperation? It is in these times that our convictions are truly revealed. Under pressure, many beliefs we thought were convictions give way to fear and we discover they were merely preferences. We have a family to consider; decisions that have to be made, children who will carry the consequences of our choices, and a faith that will occasionally be put to the test. All are very good reasons to be fearful. During these times, we need to revisit our values and goals. We need to revisit the reasons we started homeschooling in the first place. We need to look at the options that are available to us. Ironically, looking at those options can fill us with a whole new set of fears. So we just need to do it afraid

Deciding Whether or Not to Go Back to Work

When we were faced with financial crisis, a whole array of questions I thought I had solidly answered resurfaced, such as, "Do I go to work or stay home?" "What do my kids need more: financial stability or my physical presence?" "Is my husband not able to support us? Is he doing enough?" "What is God's will for our family?" "Did we make a mistake?"

I pondered these questions for a long time. I know from speaking with other homeschool moms that I am not the only one. We become fearful when we struggle financially. Difficult situations made me question what I had thought to be true. That God was our provider. That He had called me to be a stay-at-home mom. That homeschooling was the best thing for our family. We had made decisions based on these beliefs. Now I was asking myself if this season was over.

Two years into our financial troubles, we were hosting a barbecue and I was sitting with extended family on the deck of our home.

Someone at the table said, "So I heard you guys are struggling to make the house payments."

"Yes, it's been a hard time," I said.

"Well, maybe it's time you went back to work," said a family member. "I know you like to homeschool and that's great. But don't you think you need the income now? Are you afraid to put the kids in school?"

"Yes," said another. "You've done a great job. They'll be fine. You should think about going back to work."

At that moment I felt so uncomfortable I just said I wasn't finished. After all, my youngest was four. It might have appeared that I was finished because my oldest was now married, but I still had a long way to go. It wasn't just being afraid to send them to school. I wanted them to explore who God made them to be and I didn't think public school would give them the same opportunity as they had at home to do that. I didn't get into my faith reasons for homeschooling or the provision God had given up to that point, but we had seen God do some amazing things. Checks would mysteriously appear from people we did not even know. Sometimes my Bible study group would step in and give us food and an envelope with just what we needed. God was providing for our daily bread, which included utilities and gas for the cars, and I was doing some tutoring outside the home to earn some income. None of that would have mattered to them at that moment. In their faces, during this conversation, I saw what I had already been suspecting and had been afraid people were thinking. They were thinking I wasn't trying hard enough to get out of this, or that I was set on doing things my way. Now I knew it wasn't my imagination. People really were thinking that! I had given a weak explanation and defense regarding why I would continue homeschooling because I was having a hard time believing it myself. I was uncertain of what I should do. Was it irresponsible for me to not stop homeschooling and go to work?

The answer can be tricky. There are stay-at-home moms, homeschool moms, who believe it is time for them to go into the workforce. My purpose is not to convince anyone that they must continue to stay home. The question is "What do I believe is the best for my family at this time?" As Christians, we pray for God's leading in such matters. There is no easy formula that tells us how to know when God is leading us to go back to work and when to stay home, but here are a few things I have found: when I am desperately looking for a job while thinking that this will be the only way out of the problem, it's probably not God. I'm being led by my fear of financial uncertainty. When I am looking at my husband with resentment and pressuring him to do more and more when he's already working hard to provide, it's probably not God. I'm being led by my fear of financial uncertainty.

Fear of financial uncertainty leads us to see our circumstances and fear that we won't make it. We are afraid that we won't have the life that we planned to have and the things that we wanted to have. When we don't get what we want we experience pain, and no one likes pain. There is a difference between making a decision out of fear and choosing to do something because you feel convicted to do it. Have you ever had the experience of double-mindedness? You wakeup in the morning and the first thing that comes to mind are all the problems. Then you say to yourself, "This is ridiculous. There's no way we can get out of this mess without me going back to work." So you decide to go back to work. In the afternoon, you watch your children as they read or play or you see all the things that have to be done at home that you don't have the time to do and think, *This is ridiculous! I can't go back to work! I can't miss out on my kids! Besides, -I can't even finish all the housework as it is! How can I add a full-time or even a part-time job to this?"* One of your kids asks as he's going to bed, "Mom, can we buy..." or "Mom, when you go to the store, can you get me..." And you think, "This is ridiculous! Of course I'm going to have to go back to work." This is double mindedness and it drains our energy. In the New Testament of the Bible, James chapter 1 talks about double-minded people. Let's use this verse to figure out how to get out of double mindedness.

> "If any of you lacks wisdom, you should ask God, who gives generously to all without finding fault, and it will be given to you. But when you ask, you must believe and not doubt, because the one who doubts is like a wave of the sea, blown and tossed by the wind. That person should not expect to receive anything from the Lord. Such a person is double-minded and unstable in all they do" (James 1:5-8).

Following this verse I've discovered four important elements in deciding whether or not we should go back to work.

1. **Ask for God's wisdom.**

When we can't make up our mind we feel unstable. So how do we settle the uncertainty in our hearts of whether or not to go back to work? How do we know that we are not simply reacting to our fear of scarcity? When we set our mind on there only being one way for our needs to be met, we are putting God in a box. It amazes me how God provides from different places and in different ways. Just when we think we have Him figured out, He provides for us from a completely different direction than we ever could have guessed. His ways and thoughts are definitely higher than our ways and our thoughts! And if His ways are higher than our ways, and His thoughts are higher than our thoughts, then what we need is His wisdom. We need Him to lead us in our decisions. Only He has the ability to see the possibilities that we couldn't possibly imagine.

2. **Don't be so hard on yourself.**

As the verse above says, if we ask for wisdom, God will give generously to all without finding fault. That part, "without finding fault," is very important to me. Homeschool moms can be extremely hard on themselves. We take on the responsibility of everything from our children's academics to their character to their life decisions to the major they pick in college. We want the credit when things go well and we take all the guilt and shame if it doesn't. That mentality can make it almost impossible for us to make up our mind on whether or not to go back to work. After all, that decision will determine the lives of our children. They will live or die based on what we decide. Of course I'm being sarcastic. That's not possible! We don't have as much power as we think. God is not in heaven saying, "Don't screw this up, now. We can't come back from this." Or "Wow. I thought you knew better. Now what do I do?" The verse in James reminds us that God gives us wisdom without finding fault. He's on our side. He wants us to succeed. No matter what we choose, He's got this.

3. **Believe that God is working**.

"But when he asks, he must believe and not doubt…" The implication of waiting is one of my biggest challenges. If we believe, that means we wait for God to answer. The problem is that I'm a first born, what's the plan, when are we doing it, put it on the calendar, let's get it done kind of person. When I start to panic because of financial uncertainty, there are statements that make me even more nervous. They are: "Let's pray about that," "Let's wait and see," "Let's wait on the Lord,"… You get the picture. The waiting can make me anxious. (Unfortunately for him, my husband is the one who uses these statements more often than I'd like to hear them.) My response is usually, "'Till when?" "When do we say, time's up, let's move forward?" "How long are we praying?" "What exactly are we waiting to see?"

We sometimes confuse waiting with passivity, but waiting on God includes being aware that God can lead us in different ways. New opportunities may come our way. We might have a conversation with someone who may help us see things in a new light. We might get confirmation that we are on the right path, or we may have to collect as much information as we can and then set a date to make a decision. Either way there is a period of waiting but there is also expectation of what God will do in us, through us and for us.

You might be just starting off on your homeschool journey or you might have been doing it for years. Wherever you are, you are forming your own experience and your own story. I assure you, God does not play favorites. He is faithful to you. If you are in a waiting stage (and we all are at some level), just know that God is working behind the scenes to do in you a good work. Keep on doing what you believe He is calling you to do, connected with Him through prayer and Bible study. I have found that the progress through the journey is not evident or obvious in the day to day living, but in looking back to all that God has done. Write your story as it happens in a journal. Even the little things. Then go back to the journal when you're going through a dry spell. It helps you remember where you have been and remember God's faithfulness through it all.

4. Follow through.

I don't only have a problem with waiting, I also find it hard to follow through with what I believe is the next step. There are times when I feel that God is leading me and confirming His response or His leading. At that moment I feel sure God has answered. The answer doesn't come in the form of some rushed decision or a desperate running around trying to find solutions to my problems. It doesn't contradict God's Word, it's confirmed by other means, such as research, conversations with people I respect, and teachings I am listening to. At that moment, I have a clear understanding of my next steps. However, when I go on with my daily activities, I start to second guess myself. "Maybe that's not what God wants." "Maybe that won't work." So back I go to wondering what I should do. Usually when that happens, God is kind enough to remind me in prayer that He already told me what to do.

This often reminds me of the story of Moses. When he was bringing the people before the Red Sea and saw himself surrounded by the soldiers behind and the sea before him, Moses told the people, "The Lord will fight for you; you need only be still." Then the Lord said to Moses, "Why are you crying out to me? Tell the Israelites to move on."

That's the impression I get when I go before God with a question He's already answered. "Why are you crying out to me? I already told you what to do. Go do it!"

So to recap, the four important elements that are helpful to me in deciding on whether or not to do something are: 1) ask for God's wisdom, 2) don't be so hard on yourself, 3) believe that God is working and 4) follow through.

Presently, I'm at number four. I have felt God respond and lead. Now I am trying to work through the steps He's put on my heart, confident of this: if God really did put this in my heart, He will provide the way. My job is to move forward in that direction. I find that if He didn't put it on my heart, I'm still moving in the faith that He is more than able to block me, turn me around, and close any doors I shouldn't be going through.

Faith is always crucial in the decisions we make regarding financial uncertainty or anything else. In his letter to the Romans, Paul addressed the question regarding eating meat sacrificed to idols. This meat was usually cheaper in the market, and the Christians wondered if it was okay to eat it. There were also new Gentile Christians who wanted to know if it would be fine to eat at the house of a friend without knowing for sure if the meat had been sacrificed to idols. Paul responded in Romans 14:1-4:

> "Receive one who is weak in the faith, but not to disputes over doubtful things. For one believes he may eat all things, but he who is weak eats only vegetables. Let not him who eats despise him who does not eat, and let not him who does not eat judge him who eats; for God has received him. Why are you to judge another's servant? To his own master he stands or falls. Indeed, he will be made to stand, for God is able to make him stand."

Paul ends the chapter by saying:

> "Do you have faith? Have it to yourself before God. Happy is he who does not condemn himself in what he approves. But he who doubts is condemned if he eats, because he does not eat from faith; for whatever is not from faith is sin."

Do you see it? It is no use trying to decide what to do by watching what others have decided to do. I wish it was that easy! But it doesn't matter how many homeschool moms are going back into the workforce if you believe you need to stay home. Likewise, it also doesn't matter how many homeschool moms are choosing to stay home, if you believe it's time to go back into the workforce. With that in mind, the question of whether you should go back into the workforce or stay home, is more about whether you are doing it by faith and not about whether it worked for your friend!

In times when I have been indecisive about going back to work or not, one of the biggest lessons I learned was not to process outloud. When the bills were overwhelming and there was no income in sight,

I would consider going to work. When I voiced that, everyone around me would start to quietly panic. One would have bad dreams about me leaving. One would worry that I wouldn't be there when she needed me. In the end, it was all for naught. I'm not going anywhere until I get a clear direction from God. So why voice it to begin with?

I think as moms, most of us underestimate our influence. We have little idea of how much weight our words carry, how significant our presence is, how dependent our family is on us. While some moms might have too high of an opinion of themselves, I think most of us have too little. Just because our children do not rise up and call us blessed every morning, that does not mean they don't need us. They may even take us for granted, but the fact is, we are a very important part of the puzzle. The sooner we realize that, the more intentional we can be about the things we do and say, the direction we set for ourselves and the decisions we make about what is really important. What we think matters. What we say matters. What we do matters. It matters more than we think, it impacts more than we realize and it affects more people than we can imagine. The danger of grasping this reality is that we could become paralyzed with fear and be unable to make a decision for fear that we may ruin our families, but be assured you are not alone. Ask God for wisdom. Remember how valuable your presence is and how blessed your family is to have you. When I am tempted to make decisions based on fear, I hold on to the reality that I have work here that no one else can do and that has more value than any company could pay me. As of now, my work at home is too sporadic to commit to certain hours working outside the home. Perhaps sometime soon, but not now.

Glimpses beyond scarcity.

While we deal with all the ups and downs of financial uncertainty, I get glimpses. Glimpses of what God is doing in me, in my husband, in my children. Glimpses of the blessing of being home with my kids.

Silvia Escobar

Glimpses of awareness and appreciation on the part of our children for the sacrifices we made so I can be home with them (these are usually less frequent and short lived than I would like). Glimpses of solid relationships with our adult children as a result of sticking it out, waiting on God and working things out. Glimpses. Sometimes, they are my lifeline. I watch for them because they remind me that even when we don't have everything we'd like to have, God is still working in our family. They serve as a reminder that God is in control. That there is a plan. That raising a family is a process that involves more than just being able to pay for classes, lessons and expensive curriculum.

One Thanksgiving, I had another one of those glimpses. We usually have guests for Thanksgiving: a friend from one of my kids' schools who can't get home for the holidays, a family from church who doesn't have anyone else to spend it with, extended family, etc. That year it was just us, but what an opportunity. We prayed before the meal as always, but instead of going around quickly to everyone so that they could share what they were thankful for before the food got cold, my husband Arturo prayed and then we waited until everyone was finished eating. Then we took our time around the table to share. In way or another, all my children were thankful for our family in specific ways. One was glad that he always looked forward to coming home for the holidays because many of his friends didn't. Another said he liked our family's sense of humor. Another talked about our family dynamic. It always amazes me how our children can be so content, even though we've struggled so much financially, ut it shouldn't. These are glimpses. Glimpses that there is a bigger picture. That the sacrifice is not in vain. Reminders of what truly is important.

What are your glimpses? Glimpses that you've made the right choice? Being present when your child takes his first step? How about the first time they read or the excitement on their face when they show you the picture they drew? Sitting with your child and just talking? To have those spontaneous moments of conversation, we must be present. When they're younger, our conversations can be about a book they read, a friend they met, or an activity they want to do. As they get older talks might go into the night: goals, dreams, disappointments, the list goes on and on. Glimpses. Write them down when they happen. You'll need those later. When times get tough and you want to quit, when crisis comes and you second guess yourself, you'll need those glimpses to remind you that it's worth it.

Silvia Escobar

Homework for the homeschool mom.

Do you struggle with fear of scarcity? In which way?

How have you seen God's provision in the last year?

Look for the glimpses. Enjoy them. Be present.

What are the glimpses that remind you it's all worth it? (write at least three of them)

Chapter 2
What if We Can't Do Everything?

Homeschooling: Do it with the Gaps
(The Fear of Missing Out)

Homeschooling can be an expensive endeavor. There is so much to pick from. From a vast amount of publishers for every subject, to joining a co-op, to doing sports, to classes at a community college. This generation of homeschoolers has so much to pick from, but having those many choices can feel overwhelming. The pressure to do it all is real and can be very stressful. After all, we want our kids to be well-rounded (whatever that means), but what if we can't afford it all?

There is a used homeschool book sale that I used to go to every first Saturday in May. It was fantastic! I love books. I think that's probably true of every homeschool mom. I also love a good deal. If I can get them both at the same time, I feel very accomplished. I would get my list of books that I needed ready and walk into a magnificent gym with rows and rows of vendors. Aaah! Books and good deals! Sometimes I would stick to my list, sometimes I would wander from it a little, but always I would feel like I had done well. Whatever I did not get on that day, I would get at a homeschool convention I went to every year.

Silvia Escobar

As I mentioned previously, my family and I experienced some financial hardship in the middle of our homeschool years due to my husband's illness. The first year of our financial struggles I remember being very aware that the first Saturday of May was approaching. I asked the Lord to allow me to have money so I could set it aside for that day. As the day got closer, I went from asking.. ... "Lord, please provide some money for me to go to the used book sale." ... to begging, "Father, please, please, please, I need to buy some books at the used book sale." ... to reasoning. "Lord, I want to be a good steward! These are used! They're a good deal! You don't want me to pay full price, do you?"

I went from being fearful, " What if I can't go?"... to being frantic, "Oh no, I won't be able to go!".... to being downright indignant. "Do You know how important this is to me? Does anyone care?"...too justified in my anger. "Fine, God! You don't want me to get a good deal? Fine! I'll pay full price! I was doing this for You! Get the most for YOUR money! But you didn't let me. So Fine! I'll just pay full price!"

We've probably all experienced one of our children asking us for something you've decided not to give him. He is fully expecting to get it, but you shock him by saying no. Instead of saying, "OK, Mom, I know you love me and if you said no you probably have your reasons," (hah!) he follows you around while you're cooking and asks, "Why Not?," which we all know is code for "You tell me why not, and I'll tell you why you're wrong." If that doesn't work, he moves on to the reasoning, the begging and the promising. The older they are the more creative they get. Then there's the guilt; and lastly (if you haven't cracked yet), the indignant storming away with the slamming of the door behind him. Now the more he claims to need that one thing, the more he fights for it, the more it hurts to lose it, the more we as parents realize that it's reached an unhealthy level of obsession. He is holding on to it too tightly. He is probably expecting to get some satisfaction, happiness, or fulfillment from that is unreasonable to expect. I'm not saying that desires are unhealthy, it is the degree with which we hold on to the things we want that is the problem. That's where I was with curriculum.

I didn't get to go to the used book sale that year, now the convention was near. I had gone to the convention ever since we had started homeschooling some ten years before. For the first seven years of homeschooling I had not known any other homeschoolers. The convention was my yearly reminder that I was not alone. It had become very important for me to attend every year. I couldn't imagine not going, but I didn't have the money to go. At first, I started to go through the same cycle with God I had gone through with the used book sale. But I had learned from that experience that kicking and screaming wouldn't get me anywhere. Besides, I had survived not going to that sale. I didn't die, so I made up my mind to be content whether I went or not, and I purposed in my heart to guard myself from looking forward to it as I always did. Then, a friend paid for me to go. My husband and I went (spouses were free) and we had fun. We were especially grateful to be there, knowing that without my friend's generosity, we would not have been able to go, but there was no money for books.

Ever since I had started homeschooling, I had prayed that God would lead me to that curriculum that would produce the best results in my kids. There are so many options that claim to be THE curriculum that will take our children to new heights in their educational adventure. Christian ones often claim to be what the Bible says should be the way to learn. How can there be so much difference in Christian curriculum and claim the same thing? I would pray, "Lord, I only have so much time. Please, lead me to the right curriculum" (of course at the time, I had the money to buy them). Always I felt the Lord say to my heart, "It doesn't matter. Choose whatever you want," but I was always too fearful to choose "whatever

I wanted." That was too easy. I wanted God's best for my family. What if I picked the wrong one?

Have you ever walked into a curriculum fair and thought, "There are too many choices?" Well, here I was with a new feeling. "I have no choice." For the first summer in my 11 years of homeschooling I had no books for September. At times I would say to myself, "God will provide." At other times I would think, "Yes, but what does that mean? I want this list of books. I NEED this list of books. Is He going to provide THIS list of books? Because that's what I NEED!" Just like a child, I was holding on to having curriculum too tightly.

Maybe that's where you are. You're wondering how you're going to provide a quality education for your kids without any money for curriculum. You might even be wondering why you spent the money on this book when you could have gotten a good workbook for the same amount! What am I saying… you're a homeschooler… you probably got it out of the library.

That year I learned that homeschool moms do not live by curriculum alone. The library and the Internet were my best friends. I gave my kids more freedom to explore. We did unit studies from library books. I printed out worksheets. My kids learned. And we learned a lot more than just reading, writing and arithmetic.

Recognizing Opportunities.

One of the areas we grew a lot in was resourcefulness. Upcycle. Repurpose. Do it yourself (DIY): all words that mean resourcefulness. I am amazed at what my daughters can do with things we have around the house. In fact, I have trained myself to ask them if they can use something before I throw it away. I confess that it used to bother me that we couldn't just run to the store to get what they wanted. They always seem to have to find a way to use what we have to get what they want, but now that they have had so much practice I am so impressed with what they can do! In fact, my youngest daughter,

Kathy, would rather make it herself than buy it. When she does buy something, it's usually not exactly what she wants… yet. She calls it, "Escoing it up." As in, "Mom, I'm going to Esco this up and turn it into a frame." "Mom, can I Esco-up this shirt? It was in the giveaways. I'd like to make a dress for my doll." Where others see junk, my kids have trained their eye to see possibilities. That's a good thing. It's good for the environment, it's good for my guilt when I can't get them something and it's good for them. In a world that is becoming scarce with resources, it's good to know my kids will do their best with what they have. Even though we feared not having what we needed, becoming more resourceful became one of the best parts of their education. I could not have foreseen it, but God has a way of making the best out of tough situations.

This idea of resourcefulness spilled out to other areas of life as well. In the area of clothesfor example, they could not conceive buying expensive shoes, dresses and jeans. When we were able to give them money for clothes, we made it very clear that this was all they would get for the season. They got very good at stretching a dollar. Most of them chose to go to the consignment stores first to see if they could find what they were looking for. Whatever they couldn't find they would look for at the store or on-line and compare prices. I was always amazed at how much they can do with what they got. Sometimes one of them would decide that they would rather have a specific thing that would cost them all the money they had for clothes. It was hard, but we allowed them to do that since we had already made it clear that they would not get more money for clothes until the next season. This sometimes resulted in them learning a lesson on money management. Other times, it was a lesson for me since they were really good at wearing the same old clothes to have what they wanted. These were good lessons on going without and making tough choices.

Another area my family became resourceful in is food. When the budget is very limited, you need to make wise choices about what to buy. I learned a lot because of those limited choices. My kids learned to make the strangest concoctions with what we had. The second year my son Miguel was in college, he moved in with ten other guys in a house they rented off campus. They shared all expenses. For two of the three years he lived there, he took on the responsibility of shopping monthly for groceries because he had more experience in that area. He also cooked, since that was cheaper than buying frozen dinners. The guys really appreciated him and he got to eat hot, home-cooked meals.

I am sure you have read Proverbs 31:10-31. It speaks of a woman who is worth far more than rubies. I have a love/hate relationship with that woman, since she has set the standard of womanhood very high for me. However, she is a good example and point of reference. One of the things I admire most about her is her resourcefulness. "… She selects wool and flax and works with eager hands. She is like the merchant ships bringing her food from afar… When it snows she has no fear for her household; for all of them are clothed in scarlet," See what I mean? Love/hate. Resourcefulness is a gift that comes from having to do without. I do not know what kind of world my children will raise their children in, but when I am fearful that our needs are not being met, I am reminded that other preparations are going on. My children are learning to be resourceful.

I often wonder what my family would be like if we did not have unmet needs. Where would we be? What would my kids be like? I don't know, but I do know that God is also resourceful. He does not waste our experiences. "All things work together for good to those who love the Lord, who have been called according to His purpose" (Romans 8:28). I trust Him, I trust His Word, and I trust what He is doing in the lives of our children. He is preparing them in resourcefulness.

Priceless Life Lessons

My family has learned so much more than I could have ever taught them, even with the most expensive curriculum. One of my favorite examples: In my house, we watch TV (I respect those who do not have a TV in their house, but we love to sit around the tube and watch movies), but in order for that not to get carried away, we used to use TV "chips" when the kids were younger. Every Monday, they started out with a certain amount of chips. Each chip was 30 minutes of TV (I know what you're thinking. "How many chips?" It is however many you think is an acceptable amount of time for them to sit in front of the TV for the week.) When their chips were done for the week, they were done watching TV. If they had chips left over, they could turn them in for cash. Our younger four children have their birthdays in July and August. Well, come April, my children decided to watch less and less TV as they approached July. Why? Because they wanted to cash in their chips and save money to get each other birthday presents.

Now at this point let me interrupt myself, please don't picture my kids as some angel-like creatures helping each other do chores and math and skipping around quoting Bible verses. My kids fight with each other from time to time and as a family, we have a pretty rare humor that can sometimes get mean. All this to say, don't excuse the lesson, thinking, "Oh, well, that's them. My kids wouldn't do that." Well, I didn't expect it either, but it's one of the things we've learned... to work with what we have and to be grateful for what we get. No curriculum could have made my kids internalize that.

While we are in a better financial place than we were a few years ago, there are some things that I learned back then that I don't expect to change. I find creative ways to get some things I need, like bartering, buying used, going to the library, borrowing, etc, but most importantly, my heart has changed. My curriculum is no longer the answer to my children's education or success. It is simply a tool. I find myself wanting to buy other tools instead of curriculum. For example, a few years ago my children put together a homeschool magazine for kids. And as they did their research, put their pages together, and got creative, I realized we needed more computers and better programs. When I looked through a homeschool catalog and saw the price of a full year's curriculum, I thought, "Wow! For that price I could buy the computer program Isaac wanted, get David into a basketball league, some more fabric for Christy and the camera Kathy needs." These things are more long term and geared toward my children's gifts and talents. If I have money to spend on their education, that's where it's going.

One of the best experiences I had, happened during those years one day when I was most desperate to buy things my kids needed for crafts they were doing. I was so frustrated because I had very little money to work with. As I was walking through the parking lot to go to the thrift shop to look for a particular "need," I remembered a verse so clearly I knew it was sent to comfort me and give me peace. "The Lord knows that you have need of this." (Mathew 6:8) The verse is taken from the sermon on the mount, in which Jesus was talking about the needs that people have, such as food and clothing. He said that the pagans follow after these things. But, Jesus said, "the Lord knows that you have need of them." He goes on to say, "But seek first the kingdom of God and His righteousness, and all these things will be added to you." I have heard this in my heart many times since then. It is a great comfort to me, but also a great challenge, because I must then come to grips with the realization that if the Lord does not provide it, then maybe I don't need it like I thought I did.

Opportunities will be missed. No one, whether homeschooling or otherwise, gets to do everything they'd like. Compromises are made along the way. We have to choose between good opportunities and better opportunities. It's okay. Part of growing in our faith is letting some things go. "Your will, not my will, be done" is a humbling and scary statement to make. As time goes on, as I see God's provision and the growth in my family and myself, I know that this is the best way to live. Holding on to things loosely and realizing that His ways are not only higher, but better.

Surprises Along the Way

A few years ago, our family needed a vacation. We just wanted out. t didn't matter where, but we had just heard all about our friends' summer vacations and we were a little frustrated that once again we had been unable to go anywhere. Then our niece from New York called us to invite us to come and visit her. She would pay the whole thing and would take a week off to show us around. Usually, I would have said no to something like that. It would be a huge expense, no matter how resourceful we were, but I was so exhausted and desperate. We decided to accept her generous offer. It was a wonderful trip. One of the places we visited while we were there was the American Girl Doll store. My daughter Kathy had one of the older dolls, given to her by a friend who had outgrown dolls. She loved that doll, even though it was not in perfect condition anymore. Now our daughter, surrounded by all the modern, new dolls realized for the first time how much she was "missing." Well, she was a good sport. We went to all three floors and saw American Girl Doll furniture and American Girl Doll make-overs. When we got to the American Girl Doll outfits, Kathy took mental note of what they looked like and said she could probably make them. We had a good time there.

A few days later, we were at a train station surrounded by several shops. As we waited for my niece to run an errand, we saw a lottery drawing in one of the shops for the newest American Girl Doll. We could each enter the drawing by filling out a card and dropping it into the box. Well, this was one of those times when having six people in the family came in handy. We all filled a card out, including my niece. We left and didn't think about it any more. As we got closer to

Christmas, Kathy wrote out her Christmas list. She had two columns. The first one was titled, "If you can," the second said, "Can." She explained to me that the first column had items that were expensive. She knew we probably couldn't get them, but if we could, she would like them in the order they were written. In the "Can" column, were simple little things that she figured we could handle. A paint brush, some fabric, little craft tools, etc. On the top of the "If you can" list was the American Girl Doll. I looked at that list and almost cried. How could my little girl be so content with whatever we got her for Christmas, yet not lose hope? A few days later, I got a call from the store in New York. I won! I had won the American Girl Doll. I couldn't believe it. It meant so much more to me than the actual doll. It didn't matter to me that it was an American Girl Doll. What mattered was that it was at the top of Kathy's "If you can" column and God said "Yes!" That meant more to me than anything. The trip to New York and the doll were reminders of God's love and provision.

There have been many times like that. Surprises along the way. Reminders that God doesn't only care about what we need, but He wants to give us so much more than we can imagine. When I am fearful of unmet needs, I remember what God has done and I'm reminded that God cares for us and that He is for us. It pleases Him to lavish us with His love. Not only in the things we need, but in so much of what we want! Don't be afraid that deciding to homeschool will deprive you of doing or having certain things. God is aware of your needs as well as your wants and He loves you.

> "If you, then, though you are evil, know how to give good gifts to your children, how much more will your Father in heaven give good gifts to those who ask Him" (Matthew 7:11)

Homework for the homeschool mom:

Journal about the needs that you are afraid will not be met.

Most fears are unsubstantiated. They will never come to pass. Look at your fears. How probable is it that they will occur? If it is not that probable, what is that fear rooted in?

What are some resourceful solutions that you could think of to meet some of your family's needs?

What surprises has God given you along the way? They are different for every family. How are these surprises reminders that He cares for you? Write them down.

Chapter 3

What if We Make a Mistake?

Homeschooling: Do it Imperfectly
(The Fear of Making the Wrong Decision)

One of the fears we might have from time to time as homeschoolers is wondering if we have made the right decision to homeschool. I guarantee you, anytime you're having a hard day or your sister comes over with her honor student sticker on the back of her van or you tell your son to do something twenty times and he doesn't do it or your high school student misspells words you think she should know how to spell, you will wonder if you've made the right decision. I think sooner or later everyone is bound to wonder if it might have been better if their kids would have just gone to public school.

Even with all the great experiences I have had in homeschooling, once in a while I still find myself wondering what it would have been like for everyone if they would have gone to a traditional public or private school. This, of course, usually happens when things are not going well. There are bad days when we wonder, but since the next day is usually better and the doubt passes. On good days we are convinced that we are doing the right thing. Maybe most of the days are good days and we only have that doubt once in a while, but then there are seasons when really bad things happen. Seasons in life have a way of shaking us up and making us ask the hard questions. In those seasons, the doubt does not easily go away. Any good days in that season are overshadowed by the long days of trouble and pain. Those are the hard ones to overcome. The truth about homeschooling is that there will be days when you doubt and the doubt will make you afraid.

One of the biggest challenges we have had to overcome in our family has been depression. We hear about depression a lot these days. The causes are varied and we don't always know why it happens, but I do know that homeschoolers are not exempt. However, I didn't always know that.

My husband has publicly spoken for years about his personal struggle with depression and some of our children have struggled with it as well. Some of our kids have learned to manage it while others have never experienced it. As Christians, when something like depression comes into our family, we struggle to understand. Was it caused by bad influences? Was it brought on by bad parenting? Is it my fault? Why can't they snap out of it? Is it real?

Well meaning Christian friends offer opinions about possible causes: "Maybe he's just self-absorbed," "Perhaps he's being bullied," "Maybe her friends are being a bad influence," "You are experiencing spiritual attack," etc. While it may be true that depression can be caused by any, or a combination of these, or at least that these factors can contribute to the problem, in our case the diagnosis and the evidence pointed to heredity.

For many homeschool parents, when we are confronted with the reality that our child is struggling with an unexpected illness or disorder our foundation is shaken and our expectations for homeschooling come to the surface. Why are we homeschooling? How could this happen? What are the benefits of homeschooling if we are going to go through this anyway? We feel like failures. We get angry with ourselves, with our kids and even with God.

On a particular day when I was feeling this way, I was struggling with God's permissive will. I questioned why He would allow such difficult times to happen to my family if I had specifically asked Him to guide us, to care for us, to protect us. In the middle of my rant, this verse came to mind:

> "But I have prayed for you, that your faith may not fail. And when you have turned back, strengthen your brothers." (Luke 22:31)

I think of my life as a journey. Here I am, walking along a path I've never walked before, not knowing what lies ahead. Even as a Christian, reading and meditating on God's Word, the Bible, I don't always make the best decisions, but God has taught me a lot… usually the hard way. When I think of where I came from or who I was before I met Christ and the mistakes I have made along the way, I consider myself the most unlikely person to give advice. But this I can do, I can run back to where others are walking on this journey behind me and I can say, "Watch that hole. I fell in there and it took me months to get out." "Watch that rock. I stubbed my toe on it and I've been limping ever since." "You're doing great. You didn't get dirty passing that mud puddle. That's awesome."

> "And when you have turned back, strengthen your brothers." (Luke 22:31) That's what I do.

You will probably never experience the same crisis I did that made me doubt whether or not I had made the right decision to homeschool, but here is another Bible verse to consider. Jesus said,

> I have told you all this so that you may have peace in me. Here on earth you will have many trials and

> sorrows. But take heart, because I have overcome the world. (John 16:33)

"I have told you all this..." What had Jesus told His disciples in the previous verses? He had told them of how He would be leaving. How they would be persecuted, but also how they would not be alone because He was sending the Holy Spirit. The good news here was not that there would be no hard times, but that He had overcome the world. Our peace is not based on the idea of having no trials or sorrow if we believe in Him. Our peace is in Him--knowing that He is with us, and that we get our strength from Him. Knowing that whatever happens, He has overcome the world.

As I doubted our homeschooling decision, I began to realize the pit I'd fallen into on my journey up to this point in the waiting room. I was under the impression, though I never really verbalized it until then, that homeschooling was the avenue to a problem free life. What I mean by this is that I thought all those "teenager issues" out there in the public schools couldn't touch us. We were not in the public schools, we were homeschoolers. Homeschoolers don't have to deal with delinquency, back talk, disobedience, ADD, depression, etc. We homeschool so we don't have to put up with all that stuff, right? I thought so. After all, I've been to homeschool conventions. Those families running the convention all look so great. So sweet. So perfect. Yet Jesus taught us that it is not the outside we have to worry about, as much as the inside. Jesus said this in Matthew 15, when He was asked why His disciples broke the tradition of washing their hands before they ate...

> "Jesus called the crowd to him and said, 'Listen and understand. What goes into someone's mouth does not defile them, but what comes out of their mouth, that is what defiles them.' Then the disciples came to him and asked, 'Do you know that the Pharisees were

offended when they heard this?' He replied, 'Every plant that my heavenly Father has not planted will be pulled up by the roots. Leave them; they are blind guides. If the blind lead the blind, both will fall into a pit.' Peter said, 'Explain the parable to us.'

'Are you still so dull?' Jesus asked them. 'Don't you see that whatever enters the mouth goes into the stomach and then out of the body? But the things that come out of a person's mouth come from the heart, and these defile them. For out of the heart come evil thoughts—murder, adultery, sexual immorality, theft, false testimony, slander. These are what defile a person; but eating with unwashed hands does not defile them." (Matthew 15:10-20)

While it is true that bad company corrupts good character, (1 Corinthians 15:33) where does sin come from? Not from the outside in, but from the inside out. No matter where we raise our kids, no matter how remote our location or what we wear, they will still sin. They will still have to deal with temptation, because sin comes from the inside out. Sickness and disease are also part of the fallen world we live in. Depression is a result of a fallen world. I believe that the influence of the world only affects the manner in which our sinful nature and various sicknesses express themselves. The world does not produce them. The sinful nature is inside of us. For example, even though our children may experience things such as depression, eating disorders, learning disabilities, and so on, they might hear of another teen who cuts herself in order to release pain, or they may hear that drinking makes people relax, or smoking relieves stress. In their desire to experience relief, they may try these things rather than more healthy alternatives.

Viewing homeschooling as the formula that will cure or prevent any problems with our kids sets us up for failure. I've seen the disappointment over and over again, as parents like myself thought all the heartache could be avoided by homeschooling, only to find that our kids were born with a sinful nature, just like their parents. Homeschooling is not God. To look at homeschooling as the answer to our problems is idolatry. I think of idolatry as looking to something or someone to fill a need or a desire that only God or God's principles can fill. We must be careful to not hold homeschooling up to that level. We will be sorely disappointed. However, there are a few things that God can give us through homeschooling that I personally would have had a harder time seeing had we chosen another path. Things such as loyalty, togetherness and respect.

Regardless of what our family has gone through, whether it has been sickness, accidents, disorders or financial crises, our family has come together to face it together. whether they are directly affected or not. Praying, comforting, feeding, supporting. Always there, always helping, always faithful. That, my friends, is something I would not exchange for any amount of money or position. Every time I think about it, I cry. I am so grateful to God for my family. Yes, my kids have argued and been mean to each other, they've been vindictive, they've teased relentlessly, and they've driven me up the wall. My kids have hurt my feelings with their words and with their actions, and I have hurt theirs. We are not perfect, but we are united.

Now that I'm a few steps ahead, I can tell you, that that is the family I'm talking about when I say I cry with gratitude every time I think about them. I tell you this because when they were very young, I used to panic every time they fought, disobeyed, or just flat out in your face rebelled. I was filled with fear thinking I was doing something wrong and they were going to wind up in jail or in a bad marriage or flunk out of college and it would all be my fault. The result was that I took myself a little too seriously and did not always get to enjoy life as much because I was too busy worrying and being fearful!

Have you ever been too hard on your kids because they disobeyed you? When we overreact, we are usually thinking about far more than just this one incident. We are trying to stop what we believe is the "inevitable,. *This isn't him just wanting to have that cookie when I told him not to, this is him rebelling against authority and the forces of good. This is him turning his face away from God and growing up to become some ax murderer. I will not have it. I will nip it in the bud right now!* "Not only will you not have a cookie, you will not eat cookies for a month! And, you will find eight hundred verses in the Bible that tell you why you should not have stuck your hand in that cookie jar!" Well, I wasn't that bad, but I got pretty close. Fear. A horrible motivator. It fills us with doubt about our decision to homeschool. We don't see the results we thought we were supposed to get, so we think we made a mistake and we exaggerate our response.

Thankfully, crises are not the only times my family gets together. Every joyous memory also includes my whole family. I am always in awe of the fact that my children would ever want to spend time with me. Not that I am a horribly boring person, it's just that young people usually want to hang out with other young people, and while my children certainly like to do that, they look forward to our family nights together. When our oldest got married, I thought that would be it. Certainly he and his wife would not want to spend time with us. They had their own life to think about. I was so pleasantly surprised to hear when they moved close by that they wanted to come to family nights. All my children try to be here for special events like birthdays, holidays, etc., just because they want to. Sometimes they even take days off of work. My two older boys, during their college years and being five hours away from home at different times, surprised me on my birthday and mother's day by showing up. Those gifts are the best.

Then there is the respect and honor my husband and I receive from them. Again, this is not something we get from day one. This is my way of encouraging you. A reminder for when things get hard and you cannot imagine good things happening. A few years ago, our third son Isaac gave his last speech at the Toastmasters' Gavel Club he was a part of for four years. This is a Toastmasters International program that two of our dear homeschool moms have led for years. In his speech he said, "When your parents give you advice, they actually know what they're talking about. I've been blessed with really great parents, really great mentors and teachers, and I'm grateful for everything they've taught me. And I hope that I make them proud with everything I've learned." Well that was a moment I wouldn't trade for anything. My son Miguel told my husband one day when they went out to eat, that people know my husband and me because Miguel talks about us all the time. Miguel said he had professors who wanted to meet us because they knew so much about us already. On my husband's birthday one year, our oldest son Alex told my husband that he has been his greatest example as a husband and father. These are great moments. Reminders of a bigger picture. Some of us might have to wait longer than others to see them, but they're there. Sowed. Growing. Even when we don't see anything happening. It will look different for all of us, and it will probably look different than you thought, but God is working. He is always working.

It is hard to keep focused on the reality that God is always working when we cannot always see how He is working, but as you grow in your faith in what God is doing in your children, remember that every child is in process. We tend to see only the present and despair when things are not right. When I think of my children never changing, I think of a pond. A pond for the most part has the same water day in and day out. Our kids are not like a pond. Our kids are more like a river. If you stood by the side of a river and took a picture of the river and then a few minutes later took another picture of the river from the same spot, the water in the second picture would not be the same water because the river is constantly moving. Even when rivers freeze, underneath the frozen surface the river is still flowing. When your child appears to be frozen and doesn't seem to be going in the right direction, just remember that underneath God is still working. The river is still moving even if you can't see it move. Warning: During this process, when things are not going well, never lose hope in your heart. Do not allow yourself to go there. The moment our heart loses hope, we will show it in our words, in our attitudes, in our actions. We may not say, "Honey, you're just like a pond," but through our actions, through our comments, through our gestures, we will communicate that we do not believe in them. And we cannot imagine the damage we can do to our children if they perceive that we have given up on them and that we have no hope. Don't do it. After all, our hope never was in our kids or in ourselves. Our hope is in God and that He will finish the work He has started in them and in us.

It is hard to say how much of what we go through is normal everyday life that would have occurred whether we sent our kids to school or homeschooled them. We will probably never know for sure. That is why it is so important to pray for guidance when we are deciding whether or not to homeschool. We will need God's leading, wisdom and strength in the mundane and in the challenges. Overall, whatever your initial reason for homeschooling is, I venture to say that the benefits will far outweigh anything you thought they might be. That said, there will be times for some homeschoolers when the decision to send the kids to public school might be the best decision.

Choosing the Right Curriculum

One area in which homeschool moms are often afraid of making wrong decisions is curriculum. It used to bother me when I read a homeschool book from a "successful" homeschool family and I would skim through to the "how to" part. For curriculum, many of them would just say something like, "I don't want to include a list here because what might have worked for me may not work for you." I wanted the formula to get what they seemed to have. The perfect kids, the perfect family and the perfect homeschooling experience. Now I know these authors were wise. They probably saved me hundreds of dollars. So now after over 20 years of homeschooling experience, I have dreadful news for you. Please sit down. First, there are no perfect families. I know what you're thinking. "I knew that already." Yes, you did, but if we know that, why do we try to imitate them? It is good to glean from the wise. Over the years I have learned a lot from women much smarter than I am. But I am not them. More importantly, they are not perfect. You will rarely hear about their failures, sin, brokenness, trials and errors. I have had to learn that the person speaking at the conference or writing the book is a sinful creature saved by grace… and so are her kids. Just like me. Just like my kids. You probably admire something about them that you would like to have. God may give it to you, but it is probably not going to be through the same path that the other family got it because your family is unique. Again, it doesn't matter that a specific curriculum worked well for your homeschool friend. It only matters how your family is wired and what works for each of your individual children, because even among them, they are different. I know! I have six of them and still haven't run into a pattern!

Other areas related to our fear of choosing the right curriculum are questions such as Co-op or no Co-op? Sports or no Sports? Sometimes the fear comes because others are pressuring us to do things their way. Other times the pressure comes from a desire to be like everyone else. However, your family is unique, made up of unique individuals with their own gifts and talents. You cannot fit your round family peg into your homeschool neighbor's square hole. It just won't work. Even if you manage to get some of your family in there, there will be pain, frustration and anger, ecause it's not about what is working for that "successful" homeschool family, it's about what God has called *yours* to be. So pray for guidance and then have fun picking the curriculum.

Making the Decision to Send the Kids to Public School.

Now that I've told you about my struggle to stay strong in my conviction to homeschool my kids, let's talk about why some parents decide not to continue homeschooling. I have known some moms who made that decision for pure sanity's sake and the kids have been fine. I'm not saying we have to do that as soon as things get challenging, I'm just saying we need to look at our options. If you are absolutely miserable homeschooling, maybe the season is over or maybe some of the kids have to go to school while their siblings homeschool. It's not an easy decision to make, we all need to seek God's guidance on it, but remember, homeschooling is not our god. It is just one way to disciple our kids. If the kids were in school, do you think you would be a happier mom? Would the house be in order? Would you enjoy your kids more? Would you be able to function more? Do you have a challenging child that makes it impossible for everyone else to function? Are there programs available that could help him/her improve their educational experience? These are questions we all have to ask ourselves. There is no cookie cutter answer. When do our kids get the best mom they can get? Again, I'm not saying that as soon as we have bad days in homeschooling we should quit. I have news for you. There are going to be rough days whether our kids are homeschooled, go to public school, boarding school, private school or get private tutoring. At what point are we no longer able to function? When there is a long term depression setting in because we hate what we are doing or when everything is in disarray and you know it is not going to get better, it is foolish to continue doing something the same way we've been doing it and expect different results. Don't let shame, guilt, or an unrealistic dream of the perfect family that you saw on the cover of some homeschool magazine fool you. There is no perfect family. There are healthy families who homeschool and there are healthy families that have their kids go to public school. There are dysfunctional families who send their kids to public school and there are dysfunctional families who homeschool. Sometimes we need to make the hard choices that will help our family be more stable and function better.

Homework for the homeschool mom:

Remember a time when you believed that you made a wrong decision. How did God redeem that?

What are the decisions that you have made that you are afraid might be the wrong ones?

Follow the scenarios in your head to the end. For example, if you have picked several kinds of math programs and your child just does not get it, what is the worst that will happen? Will he have to take some remedial classes in college? How horrible is that? Can you see God redeeming that?

Or is it more challenging? Do you have a child who refuses to believe in God? Does your child have learning disabilities that you think might have been helped a different way? Turn it around. What are some advantages your child has experienced as a result of being homeschooled? How might it have been worse if you had not been homeschooling them?

Do you think there is a possibility that some things might change? Are you thinking it is time to send your children to public or private school? What are your reasons? What is holding you back? Are there unrealistic expectations regarding homeschooling? Are the problems you are facing unique to homeschooling or just part of living? Will the problems go away if you send the kids to school or will you be trading one set of problems for another? Do you fear making a decision because you think it will bring condemnation and shame? If so, what is the truth about God's love and mercy over your life?

Chapter 4

What if My Husband and I Can't Agree?

Homeschooling: Do it Together
(The Fear of Shared Decision Making)

Without a doubt, my marriage relationship has been the most challenging relationship in my life. One of our greatest challenges is agreeing with each other about how things should be done. We see and do things differently, and although we have different ways of arriving, we usually have the same destination in mind. We want what's best for our lives, we want to have a great marriage and we want our children to succeed. So why is it so hard to agree? I believe there are at least two reasons why we struggle in this area: pride and a need for power.

No one likes to think of themselves as prideful, and yet, we all struggle with pride. We can be proud of a personal achievement or of a person, such as our child. This kind of pride can be healthy. The kind of pride I'm referring to is a conscious or unconscious belief that we are better than someone else. We believe we are better people, more intelligent or more mature. Here is an example of the pride I'm talking about, you call your husband at work and ask him to pick up your son from basketball practice on his way home from work. As you hear your husband walk in the door the phone rings.

It's your son, who is still at the park, waiting for his ride. What are your thoughts? What do you say? If it's me, I at least think, "You always forget! You never listen. How could you not remember?" I just attributed his mistake to his character. "You always… you never… how could you…"

Now let's say your kid is waiting for his ride that never came, but this time it was you who forgot. What do you say to your kid as he gets in the car? "I'm sorry. I was cooking and lost track of time. Your sister needed help with her homework and I didn't realize it was so late." I just attributed my mistake to my circumstance.

Don't miss this. It was revolutionary when I heard it. In human nature, we tend to attribute our mistakes to our circumstances but the mistakes of others to their character. Realizing that reminds us of how prideful we are. Remember, your husband is human too, so he's probably doing the same thing to you. We are all prideful. We may not always say things that are prideful, sometimes we show it with our body language. Have you ever rolled your eyes at your husband? Have you ever folded your arms or pointed your finger when explaining why you're right? Have you ever smirked as he says something that you think is not very smart? That's pride. It is alive and well in each one of us, and it makes it hard for us to agree as a couple because each one of us believes we are right. Unless we step into humility, we cannot see the possibility of being wrong.

Being aware of our own faults and realizing how God forgives us for our mistakes is a great way to remember that we have no right to judge another person. No matter how many mistakes our husband makes, we can at least match him. Our inability to see that proves how much pride we have. That doesn't mean, however, that there are no consequences for the mistakes he makes or the mistakes we make. We need to hold each other accountable, but accountability does not shame or belittle. Just think of how God holds us accountable. He is merciful and does not hold grudges.

It is scary enough to decide to homeschool without thinking of how we are ever going to agree as a couple on what curriculum we will use or what priorities we will have. If we can listen more and talk less, if we can try to understand our spouse's point of view instead of insisting they understand ours, it will go much better. Note: overall it is not a good idea to homeschool if both parents are not in agreement. I've seen moms passionate about homeschooling feel very much alone as they try to do it without their husband's support. I've also seen moms have a miserable time of it because they feel forced to homeschool by their husband who thinks homeschooling would be the best thing for their kids. If you are not both on board, I would say wait. Again, it is hard to humble ourselves enough to listen to each other. We sometimes mistakenly equate humility with a lack of power.

Although there may be times when we or our spouse insist on having power, I believe what most of us are looking for is autonomy. We all have a need to exercise our free will, our sense of autonomy. When we do not work together as a team, when one person makes all the decisions, the other is left feeling overpowered. That goes against what God created us to be. There is a common thread throughout Scripture that I see over and over in the life of God's people: choice. When Eve ate from the forbidden fruit, she had a choice. When Cain was thinking about killing Able, God reminded Cain that he had a choice. When God spoke to Noah, he chose to obey. Abraham, Moses, Joshua, Esther, and the prophets; they all chose. The greatest example I see in the Bible of someone who chose is Jesus. In John 10, Jesus referred to Himself as the Good Shepherd. He talked about laying down His life for the sheep and how the sheep knew His voice. Then He said,

> "The Father loves me because I sacrifice my life so I may take it back again. No one can take my life from

me. I sacrifice it voluntarily. For I have the authority to lay it down when I want to and also to take it up again. For this is what my Father has commanded." (John 10:17,18 NLT)

Throughout history and still in many parts of the world, including the U.S., women have been literally beaten into submission. Many well intentioned Christian men remind their wives that they must submit because the Bible tells them to do so. Such desperate acts leave a very important part out of the equation: choice. In my desire to be more like Jesus I can see not only the power of choice, but the power of choosing obedience. Not obedience to my husband, but obedience to God. My husband and I have the same value before God, but we have different gifts and talents. I choose to be a giver. To work with my husband to come up with the best solutions for our marriage and family. At anytime I can choose to do whatever I want, but I know that doing what I want without respecting his opinion or asking for his input will only bring disunity in the relationship. Whenever I do what I please without including him in the decision making process, I become a taker and stop being a giver. Being a taker is a product of sin. God is a giver, not a taker. If I want to be more like God, I must become more of a giver and less of a taker. I must try to work with my husband not against him. This is my choice. As a result, God has always protected me. He has always provided for me, and I have found that the life I laid down, He has given back to me.

I know that it is God who ultimately provides for me and my family. This frees me up to love and respect my husband. I do not have to wait for him to earn my love or respect, I do not have to pressure him to change. I simply do what God asks me to do because I answer to Him above all else, and I hope that my husband would do the same. Seeing my life this way frees me up to give my husband the benefit of the doubt and not be afraid to sit down with him and work out a plan we can both agree on, even when it doesn't look like what I originally wanted. But it doesn't look like what he originally wanted either. It is a combination or an alternative that we can both back up and support. That's the sweet spot; when we are both being givers, not demanding, not taking.

Defining our Individual Roles

I have found that as Christian homeschool moms, we have more in common than just homeschooling. We love God, we love our husbands and we love our children. We are willing to sacrifice our time, our resources and our very lives for our children. And through it all, we want to get it right. Most of us are life long learners. We are constantly looking for godly women who can teach us to be better Christians, better women, better wives, better homeschool moms. In my case, I was a relatively new Christian when we decided to homeschool. In my eagerness to be the woman God wanted me to be, I fell prey to well intentioned Christians who were eager to tell women who they were, what their role was and what they could and could not do. The person that they instructed me to be was far from the person I was, and I mistakenly began to think that God expected me to be a silent wife who never spoke her mind or showed her character or personality. I started working on the external, hoping it would somehow change the internal. I was desperate to be a godly woman.

At one point, I wore dresses for an entire year. This would not have been so bad if I had chosen to wear them because I liked to wear dresses, but I wore dresses because I had heard that it would make me feel more feminine. It would make it easier to be a godly woman. I was told there was a verse in the Bible that said that we are not to wear men's clothes, and that somehow translated to not wearing pants that I bought in a women's clothing store. The people I heard this from seemed to be perfect. I idolized them, so I figured I would just do what they said and I'd become just like them. I remember feeling very constrained that year. There are just some things I would rather not do when I have a dress on. I remember the day one of my older boys set me free. I was sitting on the stairs, wearing a denim dress and my son asked, "Mom, why don't you wear pants anymore? You were more fun when you wore pants." Wow! I had to agree. It was not fun doing something I didn't want to do without personal conviction. If I had been personally convicted to wear dresses all the time, it would have been different. It would still have been difficult, but God would have given me the strength and the endurance to do it because He had given me the conviction. I was doing it because someone else said I needed to do it in order to be a godly wife… and I hated it. Now when I wear dresses, I enjoy it. I love wearing skirts, just not all the time. I feel feminine whether I wear a skirt or a pair of pants, because it's not the outside that changes the inside, it's the inside that changes the outside.

Sometimes the reason we are having a hard time agreeing as a couple is because we are still asking the question, "What is my role?" God desires for me to be respectful, to be loving, to be forgiving, to be gracious, to be merciful, to remember that my husband answers to God as well as I do and that God is working on him too. My husband is also called to be respectful, to be loving, to be forgiving, to be gracious to be merciful. If we are both in tune with how God expects us to treat each other, the question of roles is null and void. Why are we not asking instead, "What are our gifts and talents, and who is better at what?" and delegate accordingly? If we are choosing to serve, to be givers not takers, we don't have to fight about who's in charge. My husband and I will never be perfect at this. But with God's strength and guidance we are getting better. Before God started working in my heart, I had no desire to work with my husband and listen to his opinion. I wanted to be right, I wanted to out-shout, out-hurt, out-punish, out-insult my husband. Of course I wouldn't say this out loud (that wouldn't be Christian). I would show it in my actions, my insisting and my frustration. Now, when I do any of those things, I am convicted. I am disappointed with myself. It is in my fallen nature to point out my husband's faults, to expect him to do what I would do, because I believe I'm right and he's wrong or that my way is better. When that happens, I am compelled to ask God and my husband for forgiveness. Not because I have no choice, but because I choose to be better than that. I choose to grow. No one takes my life, I give it willingly. I am not where I should be, but I'm better than I was.

Not only are men and women unique, but as individuals we are different as well. You, as a woman, as a wife and mother are just what your husband and children need to be the people God intended them to be. They are what you need to grow as well. "As iron sharpens iron, so one person sharpens another" (Proverbs 27:17). If you pretend to be someone you're not, you deprive your family of the person God created you to be. Yes, you are in process, everyone is. God is molding your character, but your personality is formed by Him. You are not a mistake. Sweet, quiet, loud, funny, adventurous, introverted, extroverted, leader or laid back, you are wonderfully made. Celebrate it. Enjoy it. Allow God to use it for His glory and for the benefit of those around you, because if you don't, not only will you be miserable and make those around you miserable, but you will become more judgmental of others. When we do things out of guilt or compulsion, we feel like everyone else should be doing that too. It is what happened to the brother of the prodigal son. Remember the story? The older brother got angry because his father threw a big party when his brother come back. He said to his father,

> "All these years I've been slaving for you and never
> disobeyed your orders. Yet you never gave me even
> a young goat so I could celebrate with my friends.
> But when this son of yours who has squandered your

property with prostitutes comes home, you kill the fattened calf for him!" (Luke 15:29)

At this point I really feel bad for this guy. Mostly because I can relate. Every time I have done things for the wrong reasons, I've expected some kind of medal for the sacrifice. When I see someone who is doing what I "sacrificed myself" to stay away from, and this person "lives happily ever after," I have a fit. Take for example the decision I made to be a stay at home mom. I decided it was the best choice, but it was not an easy one. I was never trained to be a stay at home mom. I was trained to go into the workforce. When I felt that God was leading me to stay home, I obeyed kicking and screaming. I still remember sitting in a corner of my kitchen, crying and telling God, "I used to get paid very well for my work and people affirmed what I did. I used to get straight A's in college. I did both very well. But you have taken me out of there and brought me to a place where I don't know how to do anything."

During that time, whenever I saw a successful career woman and she appeared to have it all together I would think, "How come it's OK for her and not for me?" Secretly I would make myself feel better concluding that she had sacrificed her family for the sake of her career. She was a bad person. Of course that woman might very well be a better person than me and have a healthier family, but I felt better thinking that she didn't. When I would ask God why I couldn't have that, the answer I would get was, "You have asked me for something different" (notice I didn't say better).

I realized as time went on that God had a different plan for me. It is true that I had asked for something different. When God came into my life, we were already talking about divorce. I was working 70 hour weeks and taking some college classes at night and on the weekend. My only child at the time spent so much time at my mom's house that he called her mom (ouch)/ When I got him home he would often accidentally call me grandma (ouch, ouch). I hardly saw him, I hardly spoke to my husband, and I immersed myself in my career and my education just to get away from the reality that my family was not really a family. I came to God because I needed Him to save my family. That is what I had asked for. This is how he did it. I left my job, I left school, and I became a stay-at-home mom.

There is a movie that I've seen called *Fools Rush In*. In the movie, the guy falls in love with a girl from a totally different culture and background. He didn't expect to, but he did. My favorite line in that movie is when he is trying to convince her that he really does love her. He says, "You are everything I never knew I always wanted." That is my life in a nutshell. On my own, I would have never chosen to stay home and homeschool. I would have never chosen to be a giver to my husband and join my bank account to his, but when I took the step of faith, I found that it was everything I never knew I always wanted. That is God. His thoughts are higher than our thoughts. His ways are higher than our ways (Isaiah 55). I can look back and see clearly how He has brought me to where I am. I can trust Him with anything. I have often prayed, "Lord, I bet the farm on you. Don't let me down." Of course, He never does. He just changes my plan. His answer to me is always the same. "I will impress you again." And He always does.

Agreeing on the Budget

For those of us who have left the workforce or careers to homeschool, one of the challenges is the new financial dependence we have on our husbands. Now that there is one income, who will administer it? If I decide to stay home and he's the one working, whose money is it? Who gets to decide what we spend it on? If I'm the one doing the homeschooling, why does he get to have input on what we use and how much we spend? Fear of buying the wrong curriculum is increased when we don't have the freedom to make a financial mistake.

Silvia Escobar

The degree of health in the relationship often determines how much our finances will affect our marriage. How finances affect our marriage can often be a thermometer that measures the health of our marriage. Like any other challenge that comes our way, finances bring out what is in our hearts. When there is plenty of income to go around, there is usually not a problem. After all, there is enough for what I want and for what my husband wants, but when there are limited funds, that is when we clash. We find that we have different priorities. I have a mental list of what should be paid first and purchased last. The problem is, he has his own list. Who gets to decide? Well, if there is a history of my husband never consulting me before he makes a decision, there are going to be major problems. If I do the same, he also will not be very happy. Some couples choose not to discuss their financial disagreements for fear of conflict, but this leads to its own set of problems. Some husbands might believe that they should be the only ones with a say since they are the ones contributing income. Some women may not feel free to spend money because they don't know how much is OK and what would be considered irresponsible by their spouse. These and other attitudes and feelings show a disunity when it comes to money and also a lack of trust which needs to be addressed.

In the end it's not the money, but the health of the relationship that determines how finances will affect the marriage, so it is important to constantly work on the marriage. This way, when the challenges come, it will be the challenges against the two of you.

One suggestion I have in this area is to sit together and write a budget. Once your priorities are on paper, you are not constantly fighting each other on what needs to be done. You've had that conversation already and now you can concentrate on working through it. One of my favorite resources for this is Dave Ramsey's *Financial Peace University*. His one time payment fee to attend the seminar comes with a book, recordings of the seminar, and a lifetime membership. Anytime you need a refresher course, you can just attend again for free.

Another thing that has helped my husband and me is to determine how much we can individually spend on a whim. This is probably decided in your budget, but it is a good policy to call each other for "approval" before we spend over a certain amount.

Arturo and I decided a few years ago that we needed a new couch set. We set aside $500 for that investment. Everywhere I went I kept an eye out for that couch set. Then one day I went to Goodwill to find a totally unrelated item. There was a small crowd by the furniture section, so I went to see what was going on. They had just put a very nice black leather couch set for $500 on display! Well, it was first come, first served. There was a man on his cell phone trying to get in touch with his wife to find out if they had that money available. I called a friend so she could pull up the couch online to see how much they usually cost. She confirmed it was a good deal. The man who was there first couldn't get ahold of his wife and had to let the couch go.

I had already done my homework. I had approval, money, and confirmation that it was a good deal. I walked out of Goodwill with a very nice black leather couch set guilt free. A few things had to happen in order for this to take place.

1. My husband had to trust me to make a decision without him being there. In order for him to be able to trust me, I had to be trustworthy or, if I had made a prior mistake of spending irresponsibly, I had to have apologized and changed my way of spending. When we continuously break our spouse's trust, they feel compelled to protect themselves by questioning and restraining our decision making. With time and effort, trust can be rebuilt. Trust is a key issue when it comes to working together on a spending budget.

2. I had to be patient and wait for the right time and the right couches. There had been several times I had seen brand new affordable couches that I really didn't like. Sometimes it was hard not to settle for something I didn't like because I wasn't sure if I could get anything else for that price.
3. I had to pray for God to lead me and help me make a good choice. Praying for guidance is very freeing. When we trust God to lead us it is easier to wait for something to come along sooner or later. It also helps us not to sway on the amount we decided to pay for something.
4. I had to be willing to let it go. Even though I had approval and money, I did not have enough experience with leather couches to know whether or not it was a good deal. When I called my friend, I was risking someone else getting ahead of me, but it was more important to be wise about the purchase than to be impulsive. This in turn, increased my husband's trust in me.

Some of you may think this is all common sense, but in my experience, it is not that common. People make expensive purchases without consulting their spouses all the time, and not everyone prays for guidance when making a purchase or checks to see whether their purchase is a good one. I had to learn these things the hard way. If this has never been a problem for you, it's one less thing you have to worry about; be thankful for that gift.

Parenting together.

My husband and I come from very different backgrounds. He is from El Salvador and I'm from the U.S. from Mexican decent. When my husband's dad was going to administer a spanking, he would tell his boys to go find the twig with which to do it. According to my husband, his dad was strict, but fair--and was always the one in charge of discipline. His mom would just say, "Wait until your father gets home." In my family, my mom yelled and occasionally threw a shoe at us. She usually missed. My dad, however, was very unpredictable. His discipline was led more by his mood and temper rather than by what we had done or rules and consequences. It is no surprise then that my husband and I have such a different opinion on the subject of discipline, as you and your spouse probably do too. However, we have found that if parents do not get on the same page in this area, our children will catch on to this and everyone will lose.

For years my husband and I have seen discipline differently. I admit that sometimes I have not even known myself what I want, so I'm not sure how I expected my husband to know. For example, let's say I have a toddler who likes to play with the TV remote control. Now I have told this toddler repeatedly that he is not allowed to touch it. When he finally gives in and touches it, I give him a little smack on his behind. One day I'm cooking and I look back into the family room and see my husband watching a basketball game while my toddler is playing with the remote. I tell my husband, "Can you please take that away from him? He's not supposed to be playing with the remote." So my husband stretches out and takes the remote from the child without saying anything. I say, "Can you please tell him no and smack him on his behind because he knows he is not supposed to be playing with it." By this time my toddler has taken the remote control again, so dad snatches the remote from the child, smacks the child's behind and says "No!" Well I think that was a little rough, so I say, "Not so hard! He's just three years old!"

Or how about all the times we want our husbands to check with us before proceeding with discipline, but then wish our husbands would take more control, be more in charge, lead as the godly men they are called to be (just don't forget to check with me first). I believe that it is fear that does not allow us to free our husbands to parent our children differently than we parent them. The combination of the fear of making mistakes when raising our children and the feeling that we know better what needs to be done, leads to a fear of a husband's role in parenting. This fear compels us to unintentionally paralyze our husbands from being the dads God called them to be. After all, just like us, they will learn by making their own mistakes and they have a right to.

Here is a concept I have been learning. My husband loves our children just as much as I do. We have the same goals. We want the same for our children. But frankly, we have different approaches to meeting those goals. Often I think we are under the impression that we have different goals when actually we just have different ways of getting there. Sometimes my husband and I have to talk and come to an agreement about how to approach a situation. but other times I just need to restrain my impulse to do things my way. Sometimes I just need to let him work things out with our kids his own way. After all, they are his kids too.

Other times, it is not the way our husbands discipline that bothers us, it's that they are not involved at all. Passivity can be very challenging. The phrase I have found very effective is, "I believe it is in your best interest to…" For example, "I believe it is in your best interest to have a conversation with child X." "I believe it is in your best interest if you take initiative in this area because of this…" This gives him the freedom to decide what to do without me being confrontational. Here comes the hard part for me, I have to be willing to let him decide. At times I have also included a statement like, "… but if you don't want to have that conversation, I can do it." That's just my way of setting boundaries in situations where I believe that getting it done is more important than who does it. Now the question of whether or not it needs to get done at all is a totally different conversation. You may agree or disagree with that approach, but it helps me to free my husband without nagging him and damaging our relationship. There is no undermining, shaming, guilting, or passive aggressive tactics, which I believe are all motivated by fear. Fear that something that I believe needs to get done is not being done. Fear that our children will turn out badly and it will be all my husband's fault—fear that things will get done the wrong way, and the wrong way is any way that is not my way (ouch).

Letting our husbands be the parent is a step of faith. Not faith in him necessarily, but faith that God is working in him, us, and our children. Just as God knew what my children needed when He gave me as their mom, He knew what they needed when He put my husband as their dad. All the molding that God is doing in our character, lives, and families takes place as we do life. As we make choices. As we respond to the opportunities around us to choose who we will serve. It's all by faith.

Lastly, one of the things my husband has appreciated most about me, is that I let him know what is going on in the home when he is away. For dads who genuinely want to be part of the family, it is difficult to miss out on all the fun that goes on at home while they are away. I can say that my husband has missed out on some special moments because special moments can't always be scheduled. They happen when we least expect them, and my husband has felt the loss.

I also see it now in my oldest son who now has children of his own. He expresses sadness at missing some of the first milestones as his daughter takes her first steps in growing up. It saddens him to think of how much he might miss while he is working, supporting his family, and making it possible for his wife to stay home (which only means that he has to work harder). It is a sacrifice that I rarely think about.

I have the ability to lessen the loss of time between my husband and children by including my husband as much as possible. I schedule things for when my husband is home, set up field trips on days when he will be off of work, save the big breakfast for when he is leaving late for work. I involve him in planning family night. I encourage the kids to tell their dad what happened during the day. Or I may coach my husband to ask the right questions, "When you get home, ask so and so what he did for science today." These little things help my husband feel included and help the children feel he cares and is more than just the provider. After all, some of those children are boys. We don't want them feeling like family life is only for the mom and kids, and some of them are girls, we don't want them thinking husbands should not be involved in raising kids.

Homework for the homeschool mom:

Give an example where you have been prideful in your interaction with your husband. Are you willing to change that prideful response to see how that change could improve your conversations?

If you have conflict with your spouse due to finances, where does that come from originally? Insecurity? Lack of communication? Fear?

Is there an area in parenting that you and your spouse disagree on? Schedule a time to talk about it and come to an agreement. The next time the issue comes up you will be prepared to present a united front.

Chapter 5

What About Structure vs. Freedom?

Homeschooling: Do it Unbalanced
(The Fear of Wasting Time)

One area of guilt I always struggled with was the tension between the time spent on actual subjects like math, grammar, and science, and the time spent on self-directed interests like music, writing, arts and crafts, sewing, etc. A part of me would see my children spending so much time on those things they gravitated toward and having fun, that it didn't seem like constructive time. Surely that was not real "school time." This was compounded when my children struggled with some subjects like math and science and just wanted to get them over with so they could do the "fun stuff." Inevitably, some have gone on to college and have had to take a remedial math class to catch up, but I have come to the conclusion that it was worth it. More importantly, I have come to the conclusion that it was not wasted time.

In his sophomore year, my son Miguel wanted to spend more time on music. He had taken a few years of piano when he was younger, but when he was fifteen he wanted to learn to play the guitar we had gotten for him at the end of eighth grade. He already liked to write poems and lyrics, now he wanted to learn to write music to go with his other writings. This was also the year when my husband was sick, so in the beginning of the year I said to Miguel, "You need to do these three subjects and read these books by the end of the school year. The rest of the time you can spend on your music." Miguel said afterward that was the best thing I could have ever done for him. That year he learned a lot about music. He learned to play the guitar online. He wrote songs, but he also learned how to learn. He learned how to research. He learned how to be determined. He learned how to reach his goals. He learned to work hard for what he wanted. Miguel also learned a lot about himself. His creativity increased as he obtained tools that would help him use that creativity in more ways than before. In the midst of it, however, when I would see him strumming away at the guitar I would feel guilty and be concerned that he was wasting time; that he should be working hard at some algebraic problem, that he should be doing science experiments; that he should be preparing himself for the ACT test coming up next year. What I did not know then, was that would be his last homeschool year.

The following year, Miguel decided he wanted to go to public school to help with a Christian student led outreach program from our church. My husband and I prayed about it and decided to let him go. I prepared his transcripts for the school and the counselor told us that Miguel had enough credits so that he could graduate his junior year! Of course this was not Miguel's goal, he wanted to participate in the program for two years. So instead, he got to pick electives and come home before lunchtime. The only classes required of him were Gym and English.

After graduation Miguel still did not want to go to college, so he went to work. He tried several jobs from chef to roofer. Again, the feeling of time being wasted came to my mind. Again the fear surfaced. Perhaps you are acquainted with the effects of this fear, being bothered because your teenager is sleeping in or staying up late; being critical of the way they spend their time and their money. I did my share of nagging, stating the obvious and being critical of the friends he spent time with. I regret having given in to fear and not being silent long enough to see what God was doing. I am not suggesting that we never say anything, I am only encouraging you to wait until your heart is in the right place. When we operate from fear, our comments are less encouraging, more destructive. Remember, from the abundance of the heart the mouth speaks. When our heart is fearful, we are not very encouraging. When we are guided by fear, even the wise things we say will not be received well.

After a year of working several jobs, Miguel decided to go to college, but by this time, he had a better understanding of where he wanted to go and what he wanted to do there. He graduated with a degree in Philosophy and a minor in art, and all through college there was his music. He has done a few recordings. His lyrics are philosophical and profound. Because of his struggle with depression and possibly some undiagnosed problem with concentration, Miguel had to work very hard to get through some very challenging classes. He found that it took him longer than most others to get through the same amount of material, but he did not give up.

My third son Isaac is a writer, an artist, and a public speaker. He has been writing and drawing as long as I can remember. He writes stories, poems and songs. When he was in homeschool he logged in many hours drawing while I read to him and his siblings. He also taught himself to play the guitar and the piano. He, too, spent a great deal of school time developing all these talents. Of course when it was time for him to go to college, he wanted to go to a school that would help him excel in these areas. He's almost finished with his degree in Creative Writing. He enjoys his time at college and sees it as a tool to achieve his goals.

All of my children have a high level of creativity. They are all different, but amazingly creative. I say amazingly, because I've never considered myself to be a creative person. I wonder if that is because I was never given an opportunity through traditional school to discover my own creativity. My fourth child, Christy sewed pillows for the whole family, but they were all different, according to how she saw the person. She made her big brother Alex a pillow with the Chicago skyline and clouds and sky in the background. She made Miguel a pillow out of bandanas, which he always wears, and sewed music symbols on it. Isaac got a baby grand piano pillow. David, my fifth child got a pillow in the shape and design of a can of Mountain Dew. Kathy got a pillow with some of her favorite designs and colors. My pillow has a window with snow falling outside and embroidered letters saying, "let it snow, let it snow, let it snow." I had told her once in the middle of a snow storm that I only enjoyed the snow after everyone was safely home. Arturo got a picture album pillow with a bunch of family pictures printed out on special cloth, and Elisha, my daughter-in-law got an old fashion coffee shop shingle as a pillow. Amazing! I have to admit, though, sometimes when she was working on those pillows during "school time," I found myself wondering if she shouldn't be reading a textbook instead.

Christy is now in college and is loaded with school work. She is on a five year dual program to get both her undergraduate and master degrees. She's also very involved in leadership at her school. I'm so glad now that she had time back when she was homeschooling to use her creativity to make pillows, sew clothes, make costumes and all kinds of decorations; things she doesn't have time for now. The creativity that she fostered in those years is now helping her create curriculum for the children's ministry at our church where she works throughout the year and make little presents for friends and family.

My son David loves sports. He loves playing it, he loves watching it, he loves talking about it. He is a very practical person. He doesn't enjoy academics, so he would rather just get it done because he enjoys his free time. He likes to take control of what kind of curriculum he will use for the year and just needs me to set the parameters of what he needs to learn and to hold him accountable for doing his work. He cannot complain about the books because he picked them and he feels a sense of responsibility to finish them because that will make him feel like he accomplished what he had to do. He has played soccer, football and basketball. David has a lot of energy and sports are the best outlet for him in that area. David's creativity is in reasoning. He is quick on his feet and is very logical. Of course his quick thinking and smart responses have at time gotten him into trouble, but I believe God will continue to mold those gifts and I can hardly wait to see what He does with them.

My youngest, Kathy, is super creative. I think this is from just being around homeschooling since she was born and watching her brothers and sisters use their creativity. She's always busy making something, thinking of ways to sell her products and buying supplies for new projects. When we walk into the crafts and fabric store, she takes a deep breath and says, "The best smell in the world." She wants to be a photographer, have a flower shop, and make jewelry and all kinds of crafts. She, too, likes to get all of her "school work" done so she can get on with her "real learning."

Our first born Alex had a different experience from the rest because he had just finished third grade when we decided to homeschool. Since I did not know what I was doing, I got a boxed curriculum for the first two years. A boxed curriculum has all the subjects pre-picked for you from a satellite school. You just pick the grade you want and they send all the subjects you need for that grade in a box. After those two years we did mostly unit studies. These consisted of finding an interest that one our kids had and doing all or most of our subjects around that one subject. If you're interested in any of these methods, there are lots of books on the subject and plenty of information online.

Silvia Escobar

That first year of homeschooling was tough. I heard a lot of, "my teacher didn't do it that way!" Also, the first seven years of our homeschooling took place in Chicago, where there were no other homeschoolers to be found. Alex had a tough time engaging with other kids his age who didn't homeschool. Every time he met a new kid he would have to explain what homeschooling was. Alex did manage to finish high school in three years, making him one of the younger students in his freshman class in college. I think he would agree that one of the things we would do differently if we could do his high school years over again is to expose him to some activities that were outside his comfort zone. Alex is an introvert and more of a private person. As a result of that, he did not desire to be out with friends, go on a missions trip or anything that would have a lot of people. This made his high school experiences very limited. Instead of pushing him out of his comfort zone, we conceded to what he wanted. That was a mistake. His first year away at college was very difficult, and because he had limited experiences in high school, he was not sure what he wanted to study. As he finished his second year he decided that he was done with college. He still didn't know what he wanted to do and he rightly concluded that continuing to take classes without any clear direction would be a waste of time and money.

Even though college was not for him, it was not wasted time. Alex benefited from that experience in many ways. He would agree that the best thing to come out of that experience was that he met his future wife. They've been married since 2006 and as of the writing of this book have two beautiful little girls.

Alex is a strong firstborn. He's a leader. He has said that if he ever decided to go back to school he would major in business, although it would probably be more for fun, since he does not see the need for it now. He has found working in business invigorating at the company where he is. His boss has seen the leadership skills and the knowledge he has of computers, business and people. Because of this, he now leads the company. Most of what he has learned, he has learned without the need of college courses. He knows how to research what he needs and he takes risks. He is a successful young business man, a godly husband and father, and a son who honors his parents. He keeps a close watch on his siblings and especially encourages David in his love of sports.

Even when things don't go exactly as we planned, or we used the wrong curriculum or took the wrong classes, nothing is etched in stone. No one experience in homeschooling is going to ruin your child's life. So lighten up. Enjoy your kids. Take advantage of the opportunities to enjoy life along the way, even at the expense of not getting all the school work done for the day.

The Good and Bad of Technology.

As I mentioned before, when my children were very young we used to use a chip system. Each chip was thirty minutes of screens time. They could choose to be online, watch a movie, a thirty minute video, or play a video game. Unused chips were turned in for cash at the end of each week. Anything we were trying to promote was an exception, so watching a movie as a family would not require chips because we did not want them to be tempted to not be with the family because they didn't want to "waste" the chips on that movie. It was a "free" movie, so they enjoyed it even more! As they got older, we switched from chips to an honor system. We would step in to regulate only if we felt that they were spending too much time on screens.

Let me just say something about myself. I love technology. It simplifies my life in countless ways. I love a good movie and I have my favorite TV shows. I believe technology is amoral. It is neither good nor bad. It is how we use it that makes a difference. Frankly, while things like pornography, desensitization to violence, and passivity are valid reasons to be concerned, I believe that the biggest problem is the *time* wasted in front of a screen. When my son Isaac was around four years old, we were working in the kitchen and I sent him to get something in the living room. He left and never came back. When I looked for him, he was standing in front of the television. His brothers had been watching a program and that was as far as he had gotten. When I called to him, he could tell I was upset. He said, "I'm sorry mom, but the TV keeps me there!" What an accurate assessment. Every time we say yes to something, we say no to something else. When our children say yes to an hour show, what are they saying no to? Playing outdoors? Doing chores? Helping with dinner? Having a conversation with family? Having a friend over? Reading a book? Using their creativity to make something or compose a song? So what can we do to help them navigate through this world of technology so that they take advantage of it without wasting their time?

First, it is a good idea to have boundaries in place. Little children need precise boundaries; older children need principles and more opportunities to self manage, but there should always be some general guidelines regarding technology. For little ones, for example, we as parents should agree and convey to them what they can watch, when they get to play video games and for how long, what kinds of video games they get to play, will they be allowed to have a computer in their room and what kinds of parental controls to get. For older kids who we are trying to teach self-management and discernment, we must also talk as parents and agree on things such as whether we consider technology a right or a privilege. If it's a privilege, when do they get to use it and when do they lose it? What are the rules for the phones? Do we use them at the dinner table? How about driving and texting? How will we know if their conversations are sound? What will be our measure, our standard? These are all good conversations to have, first with our spouse and then with our children. Don't assume your child knows the difference between right and wrong when it comes to social media and technology. Often the line is not clear. Constant conversations, a healthy relationship and accountability are the best defense against those things we fear in regards to technology.

Second, it is good to help our kids set goals and deadlines. I believe this is a priceless skill that they will always need. There are countless books written on this subject. Why? Because so few people know how to do it. Helping little ones set even a one day goal or helping our teens set a three year plan for school, will give them the tools to do it on their own some day. It also gives us the opportunity to remind them of those goals when they want to watch a movie or sit in front of the computer all day. One of my boys was once struggling with a decision of whether to go to an activity with some friends or stay home and watch an important game on television. I reminded him that watching the game would be watching someone else do life. Going to the event would be living his own life. I think those are the things they have to be reminded of.

A third way to help our children not spend too much time immersed in technology, is to keep them busy. When our kids are distracted with real life, they forget about the passive entertainment television can provide. As parents, it is easy to take things away like television, video games, and social media, but what are we replacing them with? It is our job to provide an atmosphere where it is easier to walk away from things that are not the best use of time. We live in a sedentary, yet hard-working world. The result is that we are always working, always cleaning, always doing errands. When we are done, all we want to do is sit and rest. Technology becomes a passive way of just relaxing. There's nothing wrong with that in moderation, but our kids have a lot of energy stored up inside them that needs to be put to good use. If we are not careful, the sedentary life forces them to release that energy in destructive ways. After being on the computer all day, teasing and disrespectfulness are often just bottled energy ready to explode! Energy that has not been given a healthy outlet.

Lastly and most importantly, as in every other area, we must lead by example. I have often been the one to turn on the television. Or my husband has gotten home from work and has sat on the couch to watch some sports. When I say I watch television, I mean I watch it while I'm ironing, or I have it on in the background while I'm cooking. I rarely get to see something in its entirety. However, because the TV is on children inevitably wander into the room and sit down to watch what's on. Whatever they had planned to do or whatever they were in the middle of, stops because I turned on the television and the television keeps them there. Not good.

Remember, technology is amoral. While it is good to be aware of the potential dangers, it is also good to see it as a source of information, opportunity, and entertainment. Sometimes, when school has been a disaster and everyone has been on the verge of tears (especially me), I have been known to stop everything and say, "How about we just stop here for today and watch a movie?" Everyone cheers, we get the junk food out, and we cuddle in front of the TV as I chose to save the relationships rather than fight and argue with everyone. I did this in moderation, otherwise they would learn to run to passivity every time they faced hard situations. Right now I cannot remember the last time I did this.

As the kids have gotten older, they have their own deadlines and they know that a day off can cost them more in the long run. but in its time, it used to release the tension. It changed the subject. It brought us together. Another thing we do is reward hard work or a long day with a relaxing time watching a movie together. We do not have to be afraid of using technology to our benefit. As parents we have to decide what is best for our own families. Some homeschool families would rather not have any technology in their home, and they have strong convictions which should be respected. Personal conviction is what should lead us in our decisions, not fear or condemnation. Do not let yourself be pressured into doing, or not doing, something because others are doing, or not doing, it. Be gracious to others who think differently than you and be careful not make prideful comments to them.

Homework for the homeschool mom:

Do you feel like you and/or your child are wasting time? In which way? Is it really time wasted? If so, how can it be redeemed?

What has been your definition of success? How flexible are you with that definition? If your child does not meet that definition, how will you respond?

What is your view of technology? Does your view clash with your children's view? Is there Biblical basis for your view?

Chapter 6

What Will People Think?

Homeschooling: Do it Anyway
(The Fear of Embarrassment)

I have a friend who would tell me that she was constantly attacked and put down every time she mentioned she homeschooled her kids. She is one of the sweetest people I know, so I couldn't imagine why someone would attack her on her choice to homeschool. I asked her once, "How do these conversations start?" She replied, "Well, usually someone will ask something like, 'So how are your children doing in school?' That is always easy, because all I say is, 'Oh, fine.' But eventually they ask enough questions that I have to admit that I homeschool my kids. They start praising the public school system and questioning my family's decision to homeschool, and ask the question about socialization. It's bad."

Although I've run into some of that in the past, I couldn't understand why it happened to her so often. Then one day, our families attended a church picnic together. We were sitting at a picnic table minding our own business, when another woman approached us. I don't remember how the conversation started, but the questions the woman asked were directed toward my friend, so I just listened. It happened just as my friend said it did. The woman started questioning everything about homeschooling. She had a tone in her voice that said, "You have no idea what you're doing." At this point I became more than just a spectator. I interjected and left the woman considering the possibility that homeschooling might be a good idea.

That experience helped me understand my friend's dilemma. There was no conviction in her voice. No certainty. She was feeling inadequate and it showed in her answers. I remember feeling that way when I started homeschooling. I felt I had to give an explanation for my decision, especially to my extended family. It seemed that the more I explained, the more vulnerable I became. Certain people just see those times as a perfect opportunity to tell you what you should be doing. I'm not saying we should reverse the situation and tell people they're wrong to send their kids to public school, that would mean we want to be the bigger bully, but we should be confident in what we are doing. After all, we are acting on a personal conviction. That conviction gives us confidence that we are doing the right thing for our family. However, some of that confidence comes over time. As we begin to see the benefits of homeschooling and as we break off of the mentality of homeschooling being just another way to do public school, we will gain more confidence. We will see God's hand in it. We will see the benefits that go far beyond just academics. When we are trying to defend homeschooling with non-homeschoolers, we are talking on different wave lengths. That's why we can't agree. It reminds me of a conversation I once had with a salesperson.

I once walked into a cell phone store. We were looking for a good family plan and were investigating different options. As I talked to the sales person, I felt that my quest was very simple. Find an affordable, reasonable family plan and get a good deal on regular cell phones. I saw a phone I really liked and just wondered about the price. I called over the sales person. As we spoke, it became evident that we were not communicating well. It went something like this.

I asked, "So, how much is this phone?"

"Oh. You can get that phone with only $50 down today," she answered smiling.

"Well how much is it in total?" I insisted.

"If you can pay $50 today, it's yours," she said.

"Okay, but what's the price of the phone?"

"You could pay $50 today and the balance would just be added to your monthly phone bill."

"No," I started to get a little irritated. "If I wanted to pay for the phone today, without any easy payments, if I never wanted to deal with the cost of the phone again, how much would I pay?"

"Well, the price of the phone is $500, but that wouldn't be your price today."

Not my price today? What does that mean? It means that the store is operating under the assumption that I want this nice phone, but I probably can't afford the price right now, but they are in the business of giving me what I want right now. I only get to see $50 leave my hand. In my mind I will think I only spent $50, but my monthly bill will include the other $450. Since I never actually transacted that money, I would have a brand new, modern cell phone that felt like it only cost me $50. This mentality is so embedded in our culture that if you ask someone a simple question like, "How much is it," they automatically assume you're asking, "How much is the minimum I have to give you right now to take it home with me?" It sounds ridiculous. Right? Now let's go to a similar flaw in thinking, but this time it's a conversation about homeschooling.

A friend finds out I'm homeschooling. Here is a sample conversation.

"Oh! You can do that?," she asks rather shocked.

"Yes, they're my kids. Actually, I've been doing it since they were born, and you've been homeschooling yours since they were born, too! Only you don't call it homeschooling," I laugh.

"No," she says, "I mean legally. Are you allowed to homeschool your kids?"

"Yes," I answer, having gotten a better picture of where she's coming from. "It is legal to homeschool your own kids. When you think of it, it makes sense. After all, who has a more vested interest in your children's education than you do?"

"Well that's true, but what about testing? How do they know you're doing what you're supposed to?," she insists.

"Well, we have goals as a family that we want to meet. Those are our measuring stick as far as how well we are doing, but since there is a system to follow, if they want to go to college, they take the ACT or SAT, and whatever else they need, to be able to reach their goals."

"What about socialization?" (People always ask this question in a tone that indicates that surely you have never considered it and no one has ever asked it before).

"Actually, being socialized is more than being able to sit in a room with 30 other kids your own age. It's about being able to 'socialize' with different age groups and have conversations that go beyond what pop culture dictates. It's being able to ask the librarian where you could find a book, or being able to write a letter or email asking for information on something that interests you. It's about including others who are feeling left out and being able to have a conversation, not only with someone your own age, but an elderly person or a pre-schooler."

"I guess that's true," she concedes, "but what if they don't get into college?"

At this stage of my life, I have four who have finished homeschooling and have gone onto college, so this question is easy for me now, but it wasn't always. Here's the point,.this friend and I are operating on two different levels. She is coming from the standpoint of the education system; I am coming from a lifestyle point of view.

For me, homeschooling is more than academics. In fact, if I was just looking at it from an academic stance, homeschooling is super easy! Just get a boxed curriculum, fill in the workbooks, check the answers, and move on to the next week. But homeschooling is so much more! It's about discipleship. It's about training a child in the way he should go. It's about helping them discover their gifts and talents and looking for ways for them to express those gifts and talents. It's about helping your kids find what they want to do with the rest of their lives and how God can use that desire. So whether you use a boxed curriculum and get the academics out of the way to leave room for the "fun" stuff, or you use a unit study approach to pursue interests, or focus on character development, homeschooling is so much more than academics. Like the cell phone sales person, we have been conditioned to think that education is just about academics, but when we can cross over to the bigger picture, when we can take hold of the opportunities that await a homeschool family, then our conviction becomes stronger. Our understanding of this blessing gives way to passion, and our passion comes out in our conversations. Our conversations become more about helping the other person see the bigger picture, so that they too can minister to their own children. We are no longer on the defensive. We are on a mission. A mission to lovingly help others see the possibilities that await them if they dare to see things differently.

Invest in Discipline

"I am so impressed with your kids," a friend said to me. "I have seen them sitting in the church service. When they start turning to look at their friends, all you do is look at them, twirl your finger, and they turn back around! I've never seen anything like it. When I have kids, I want them to be like that. How do you do it?"

I wasn't really sure what she was asking. My kids were not angels, but they were pretty well behaved. When our family started growing, we figured we'd better work on discipline or they'd out man, out maneuver, and out smart us! So we worked a lot on discipline. It wasn't perfect and we made a lot of mistakes, but we took the time. What she was seeing was a result of lots of walking out in the middle of the service with a crying baby, reminding a toddler about what we had talked about on the way to church, walking out of grocery stores and not buying a certain toy because the child had a fit in the middle of the isle. There were some days I would cry on the way home from church because I didn't get to hear any of the service and I was exhausted. But we persisted. Eventually, they all got it. They could sit still during a service. I could leave them with older siblings at home and they would be fine. So not being sure how deep of an answer she wanted, I said, "Well, we discipline when necessary."

She was shocked! "You mean you spank?"

"That's one method we used very early on, but mostly there are consequences to their actions."

"Oh. I don't think I could ever do that."

"Well," I answered, "that's what we did."

It is fascinating to me how institutions all around us are more than happy to tell us how to raise our children and warn us to never go beyond time-outs, but they want to hold parents responsible for raising irresponsible and self-centered adults.What did they think was going to happen?

Discipline is necessary in order to to be able to function as a family. Chaos takes all the fun and joy out of being with our kids. If they don't obey, if they are disrespectful, we are going to be embarrassed when we go out in public or when people come over to our house. In our experience, the best kind of discipline is the discipline that goes hand in hand with relationship. When we establish a good relationship with our children by listening to them, spending time with them, playing with them, laughing with them, etc., they know that we love them. Even though discipline is never easy, they will eventually come to understand that we enforce the rules because we love them.

In order for discipline to work, we must have boundaries. Boundaries are lines that should not be crossed. We usually call them rules. When I was growing up, we had what I would call "unwritten rules." Of course, my parents had not read Dr. Henry Cloud's book *Boundaries*, so they did not know the importance of putting down clear boundaries. The result was that I wasn't always sure what were the rules and when I had disobeyed them. Some, of course, were obvious, not because they had been specified, but because my parents would make certain comments that led me to understand that a certain action would not be looked upon kindly. Unwritten rules are difficult to follow. There is no set line, there are no specific consequences, and this leads to uncertainty.

Before I give the following example, let me just say that I do not put people and animals at the same level. I believe that humans are created in the image of God and therefore are different from animals, but when I heard the following instructions, I couldn't help but think of some of the ways we are alike. A few years ago, we temporarily moved into a house with an invisible fence. We had a very energetic dog that liked to bolt out the door sometimes, so we were anxious to find out about the fence and how it worked. We were told, "You need to train the dog to learn where the boundaries are. You need to put flags up where the fence is, so she will hear the beep on her collar and know that if she walks further, she will feel a shock. It's more like a vibration, but it scares the dog. Gradually, she will learn where the boundaries are and she will respect the boundary. HOWEVER, if you do not train her to learn where the boundaries are, one of two things will happen. If she's a shy dog she will never leave the door, for fear that she could get shocked at any moment. If she's a bold dog she will accidentally cross the boundary, get shocked for a moment, and then realize that on the other side of the invisible fence there is no shock and since there is also a shock for getting back in, she will not come back." When I heard that, I thought, "Wow. I can learn so much more from that than what to do with my dog."

When our children know where their boundaries are and what they are allowed to do and not to do, we will know as the parents that the boundaries are clear. One way the boundaries get fuzzy is when they are not enforced. When Miguel was about five years old, I told him he couldn't do something he wanted to do. However, he continued to follow me around and insist that I let him do it! Finally I turned to him and said, "Miguel, why do you keep asking, if I already said no?" He looked at me as if I had asked the question with the most obvious answer. "Because sometimes you change your mind." That was an eye opener. Here was my five-year-old telling me something I hadn't even picked up on about myself. Sometimes I didn't enforce the boundary, so the boundary had become fuzzy.

Other times, the boundary is fuzzy because sometimes we give consequences and sometimes we don't. My kids know better than I do what my "can't come back from that" line is. Take, for example, the popular countdown. "You better be here on the count of five. One... two... three..." What would happen if we taught our kids that there was no countdown? Who said there had to be a countdown? How about just, "Honey, we're leaving in five minutes." Five minutes pass and, "Honey, time to go." Or, we are at the store and the child runs to the toy section. You call from the main aisle and say, "Honey, let's go." So what happens if he doesn't come when you call? We leave the cart, move toward the child… oh wait. That's their cue. They start moving toward you. but TOO LATE! Whatever consequences we had set beforehand are now in effect when they don't come when we call. If it means leaving our shopping for another day, then we leave it for another day. We can also stipulate beforehand that if ever we are in a place where we cannot enforce consequences right then, they will receive them when we get home. This is what I did when my children were younger. The hard part of this was that things got better and we were all having a good time by the time we got home. Coming to the child and reminding them that they still had a consequence to the earlier behavior was not easy, but if I wanted to make the boundaries clear, I had to carry them out. Warning: we are living in a child centered world. Be careful of what you choose to do in public. People are quick to judge and get you into a lot of unnecessary and uncalled for trouble. When my children were very young, I had a rule that they had to sit still in church. If they did not, there would be consequences at home. Of course I was talking about outright disobedience, not the accidental kicking of the front chair or a little squirm here and there. One day, one of my children had been horrible. During the service, I reminded him of the consequences. As we were walking out of the service, he started calling out from behind me, "Are you gonna hit me when we get home? Are you gonna hit me when we get home? Are you gonna hit me when we get home?" We had a few heads turn our way. It was a little embarrassing. Especially since the consequence that day involved not watching the cartoon he was looking forward to after church.

As a family, we are able to laugh about those things now because they were not disciplined in anger or revenge. I have seen parents out in public get so irritated with their children that they pinch them, smack them or verbally abuse them. There is no need for that when there are boundaries. That method of discipline only leads to resentment and rebellion. Now my kids have the privilege of being shocked and critical when they see children at the store throwing tantrums and parents taking a more passive approach. They are also quick to point out the entitlement mentality and immaturity in some of the teens and young adults that they encounter. Far from feeling mistreated, our children consider themselves part of the elite few whose parents cared enough to discipline. This doesn't mean that our children always do what's right. Different seasons require us to revisit our boundaries and rules. In the season I am right now, my challenge is getting the teens that still live at home to pick up after themselves since they are hardly home. They all work and have classes outside the home and have different schedules. A chore list no longer works, so I need to tweak the responsibilities at home to meet our present needs.

Sometimes the problem is not that we don't discipline, but that we discipline too much. For the first few years of parenting, my default mode was "no." I don't know why, it just was. When my kids wanted something, my mind went to "I don't think so. Why should I say yes?" Over the years, the Lord has taught me that His answer to me is usually "yes," unless there is a good reason for saying no. He enjoys giving good gifts to us. Why would I withhold good gifts from my kids? My default mode for many years now has been "yes," unless there is a very good reason to say no. Sometimes when people are broken, they like to say no because they secretly enjoy the power, but as parents, we are to look out for our children's good, not to lord it over them. We certainly do not want to get our identity from exercising power over others. When we are too authoritarian in our discipline, our children become rebellious. They feel that they can never measure up so they stop trying. This will give us the same result of disobedience as not having rules at all, leading us to be embarrassed when they disobey in public.

In that same spirit, one of my challenges in parenting is to not set boundaries just because I am feeling personally threatened. Part of the challenge of parenting is that we are always growing, learning, and dealing with our own issues, all while teaching our own children, helping them grow, and guiding them through their own issues. I have sometimes felt threatened by my children's desire to spend a lot of time at friends' homes, instead of home with us. Jealousy begins to set in and I am tempted to make up all kinds of rules that will keep them home. There needs to be a healthy balance between time with friends and time with family. While we navigate through that balance, here are some warning signs we should be aware of. Whenever the relationship with their friend or even their friend's family gets in the way of continuing a healthy relationship with our family, it's time to interfere in that relationship. I find it best not to approach the situation in a threatening or shaming manner such as, "Why do you like spending more time with them than us?" or "You just want to be with your friends." Remember we want to maintain the relationship with our kids and we want them to want to be with us not feel guilty when they don't. Perhaps it is an opportunity to take a good look at ourselves. Are we all work and no play? When we speak, what comes out of our mouths? When our kids look at us, do they get the idea that we genuinely like to spend time with them? When we have family night, are we considering the ages and likes of our children? A little competition sometimes keeps us on our toes.

Other warning signs could be seeing a negative change in our children; in their attitude, their vocabulary, their manners or anything else we highly value. This, too, must be approached with care. Attacking the character of their friends generally brings a negative reaction from teens. Conversations in which we help them see for themselves the bad choices their friends are making are best. In the meantime, it is an opportunity to enforce rules of respect. When the boundaries and consequences are clear, our kids won't feel that we are picking on them. We are simply being consistent.

With the financial limitations we had the last few years, one of the threats I personally felt was when extended family and friends were able to provide opportunities for our children we could not provide. When this happened, I sometimes stepped in and asked the other family to speak to my husband or myself before offering that opportunity to our child. It may not be something we want our child to do, even if we could afford it. We have to be careful not to allow discontent to set in our children's hearts. When other people step in to provide for our children, it is best they do it through helping the parents instead of the children, lest the parents start to lose the hearts of their children to people who appear to have a better life. The problem is that people sometimes give to children out of their own need for love and loyalty, and they really are trying to gain the heart of the child (even if they can't identify this at the time). These are times that we must step in, even if what the child is receiving is something they really enjoy or need. God will provide what they need without threatening the parent/child relationship.

It is normal to feel embarrassed when our children do not listen to us in public or when they do not honor us as parents. It may even be embarrassing when they grow up and move out to tell friends that our kids haven't visited or called. Although our children will need to make their own choices about how involved they want to be with us when they leave home, the time that they are home is a great opportunity to discipline them, to nurture a relationship with them and to balance the amount of time they spend outside and inside the home.

Embracing your Child's Uniqueness

Sooner or later, every mother finds herself in the same situation: the moment she realizes she cannot control everything her child does. It doesn't happen over night. It starts with little things like the clothes they pick, or the hairstyle they want, or the way they like to keep their room, but it might not really hit you until you hand over the keys to the car or she goes away to college. For most of us, if we do not detach our identity from the decisions our children make and if our expectations were near perfection, we will feel all kinds of emotions: guilt, shame, embarrassment, hurt, etc.

When one of my sons was around fifteen years old, he decided to let his hair grow. We were OK with this, since we had already gone through the long hair thing with his older brother. However, the oldest had straight hair and used to wear it in a ponytail. This one had curly hair, so it went wild. His jeans were baggy and he liked to cut the sleeves from some of his shirts and use them as vests. All those changes seem to have happened in one year.

I have already mentioned how every year my husband and I made preparations to go to the homeschool convention in our state. We hade been going since we started homeschooling. Whenever one of our children became a teenager, we took him or her along. At the end of this particular year, when my son had made all these transformations, he would be going once again to the convention with us.

For weeks I agonized over what people would think when they saw us. For years I had tried to fit into the "perfect homeschool family," which I thought had a different dress code than my son's at that time. I did not want to be different. I wanted to be a "successful homeschooler." Someone whose family consisted of a strong husband who led his family without fault; a wife who was always submissive; wise sons with short hair, casual pants, and collared shirts; daughters with long hair, dresses and no make-up.

Instead, here I was with my long-haired, loose pants, torn shirt son. As I realized how much it was going to bother me, I did not like what I saw in me. I had to take a hard look at myself. I love my son. I love who he is. I enjoy his company. Yet I was embarrassed-not for him, but for me. I was so concerned about what others would think, I was willing to consider not going at all. As I prayed, the Lord reminded me of the story of David. Samuel had set his eyes on Jesse's sons and had his own ideas of who looked like a king. But God looked at the heart. I was reminded that it is not the outside, but the inside that matters to God. We did go to the convention that year, and those two days were a great lesson for me. I watched people as they looked at my son and wondered what kind of person he was. Then I watched as people were shocked to see him holding the door for them. He would just stand there and smile at them as they went through. They would say thank you, sometimes with a look of confusion on their faces and I smiled. We were all learning a lesson.

Some of the biggest lessons I have learned have been the ones where I can see the connection between God's parenting and my own. For example, one of the things that brings me peace and helps me look at difficult circumstances with a hopeful eye is the belief that God is for me. He is on my side. He cares for me. Knowing this truth makes all the difference in the world. Without knowing that He loves me unconditionally, everything would fall apart. I wouldn't be able to trust Him. I'd be afraid of what He would do next. I'd feel alone and abandoned, in the hands of a whimsical god.

The importance of that truth makes me realize how important it is for my children to know that I am for them. That I am on their side. That I care for them no matter what they look like, how they dress or what they do. It is this truth that helps them accept rules and consequences. It helps them accept difficult circumstances and hard conversations. It helps them enjoy their relationship with us. If they had to worry about what we would think of them if they expressed their uniqueness, if they were not sure that we loved them unconditionally, everything would fall apart. They wouldn't be able to trust us. They'd be afraid of what we would do next. They'd feel alone and abandoned in the hands of whimsical parents.

I don't just blindly believe that God is for me, I see it in the sacrifice of His Son; His generosity, mercy and grace. So I ask myself, "What evidence do my children see that says that I am *for them*?" Do they see kindness? Love? Generosity? Mercy? Grace? It is not enough for me to tell them that I am for them. I must show it. Every time they mess up, every time they stick out because they are different, every time they appear to not have it all together, that is when they most need me to show them that I am for them. Even when I need to discipline them, they should be able to see that I discipline them because I love them. They may not choose to see it at the time, but there should be evidence that they cannot ignore, and knowing that I am for them makes all the difference to them.

Parenting is a growing experience not only for our kids but for us as well. We think we have to have everything figured out in order to raise our kids right. I think the bigger challenge is admitting we don't have all the answers and being willing to let God raise us as we raise our kids. My children are a big part of what I need to make me into the person God wants me to be. He uses experiences like the convention to challenge me to be a better person than I've been; to become more aware of my own prejudices, to see things like He sees them, and He's not finished with me yet.

All parents have a picture in their head of what "good kids" look like. When our expectations of that picture are not met by our children, it is easy to become embarrassed. When that happens, it is good to ask ourselves where our expectations come from. It might be that you have adopted others' ideas of what a good kid is supposed to be like. In order to discover the root of the embarrassment effectively, start by evaluating your own beliefs. Remember that God looks at the heart. Is what your child doing a matter of right or wrong or just different from what you expected? Perhaps your own desire to please others or look good in front of others is causing you to put pressure on your child. What a great opportunity to grow as a parent.

Silvia Escobar

Homework for the homeschool mom:

Why did you choose to homeschool? Did you choose it because your child was being bullied at school? Were you following in the footsteps of someone you admire? Did you have a romantic view of homeschooling? Most of us started for one reason and discovered more profound reasons to continue. Is it time to change it to a deeper reason?

Is there something about your child now that is causing you to be embarrassed? Why do you think that is? Is this perhaps an opportunity for you to grow?

Chapter 7

What if I Can't Do This?

Homeschooling: Do it One Day at a Time
(The Fear of Responsibility)

There are so many emotions as we approach the ending of our homeschooling with each child. Is he ready? Did I do enough? What if she can't make it? If you have a child who is close to finishing or has already graduated, you might have had this experience already. Like some TV sitcom, you imagine watching your child in college, sitting in the middle of the classroom. The professor asks a question that all the students know the answer to. All the students, that is, except your son. All eyes focus on him, as the professor says (in slow motion), "He doesn't know because he's homeschooled! And IT'S ALL HIS MOM'S FAULT! It's every homeschool mom's worst nightmare, and yet, so against all the research that has been done about homeschooling. Homeschoolers are winning spelling bees, they're responsible, they have excellent character, they have high ACT scores, etc. Ironically, though, sometimes these statistics only serve to make us more nervous. What if my kid can't spell? What if their ACT score wasn't that great? What if they can't even keep their room clean? The sense of responsibility can be very overwhelming. Am I really responsible for all that? Can I handle it if I am? What if…?

The more important something is to us the more fearful we become at the weight of its responsibility. So, of course, fear the responsibility that comes with homeschooling makes perfect sense. Because of this, we are not easily convinced that everything will be fine just because we hear success stories or are told to have faith. In fact, many of us will not be convinced until we start to see the fruit of our labor for ourselves. This is because each family is unique. Your family is not like mine or like anyone else's. Examples you hear may or may not relate to your situation. In fact, some examples might make you more nervous! I recently saw a post online from a fellow homeschooler encouraging friends to read an article about a homeschool family whose children were all finishing college at age twelve! How is that encouraging if you're struggling with Algebra 1 and your student is already sixteen?

The longer I homeschool, the more relaxed I get. That's because I've had the experience of seeing four of my six children get accepted into the college of their choice without having been academic geniuses. As I've homeschooled, I've looked for opportunities for my kids to excel in their strengths. This decision has been at the cost of high ACT scores and a strong understanding of math. I have no doubt that if I would have concentrated on them getting a high ACT score and sent them to a math tutor, they would have achieved that instead. There might be homeschoolers who can handle both things, but in my family, our resources and time have been limited and we decided to invest those resources in their strengths. Yet, this has not stopped them from getting into the college of their choice! The worst that has happened so far is that some have had to take a remedial math course in college.

At the end of the day, we are responsible for our children whether they are homeschooled or educated elsewhere. Neither is foolproof, neither is perfect. The question is, do I believe God is leading me to homeschool or not. Some of the comments people say when they find out I homeschool reveal a misconception of our responsibility and position as parents. You've probably heard them too, "Wow. I could never do that," "I don't have the patience," "My kid would never listen to me," "You're super mom," but homeschooling is really just an extension of our responsibilities as parents.

Let's look at these comments one at a time. "I could never do that." God often calls us to do a lot of things we cannot do on our own so that we can depend more on Him. In fact, I always feel we are in a better position to succeed if we feel we can't do it than if we think we can. It is in understanding our need to depend on God for our success that we really receive the ability to do what we are called to do.

"I don't have the patience!" Who does? In the Bible, the letter of James tells us in chapter one that patience comes through hard times. There certainly are hard times when our family is in the same house 24/7! Patience is something we acquire as we go. When I think about the things that caused me to fear before, compared to what causes me to fear now, I see how God has been molding me all along. If we never allow our patience to be challenged, it will never grow in us.

"My kid would never listen to me!" Well, that says a lot, doesn't it? Homeschooling is more than an opportunity to teach our children reading, writing and arithmetic. It's an opportunity to mold them spiritually, morally, and in character. Obedience is essential for an enjoyable homeschool experience. I would say that has to be put in place first, but it is just as important if we send them to someone else. What public school teacher wants to be teaching kids who are not disciplined? One of the reasons why discipline is so challenging is because it is ongoing. Every season brings its own challenges. Kids get older. Circumstances change. Rules need to be revisited. Boundaries are always tested. For us, a sense of respect and obedience are one of the biggest priorities in homeschooling. Society will thank us and so will their college professors and future bosses.

Silvia Escobar

"You're super mom!" This one always makes me feel good… and awkward, because the truth is, I couldn't do it without God. While you might feel sometimes that the burden of responsibility for your children's education falls on you alone, the reality is that when we rely on God, He will lead us. In my experience, the trick is to hold on to our expectations loosely as we work hard to carry out our mission as homeschool moms. The result might not be what you had in mind, but God is never taken by surprise. He uses everything, good and bad, to mold our children into the people He wants them to be.

Walking Them Through Their Faith.

Guiding my children in their faith has been one of my fears of responsibility. When my kids were little, it was a lot easier. I would read Bible stories, we would have family devotionals, we would pray together, and we would take them to the children's ministry at church. As they got older, it became more challenging. We wanted them to do their own devotionals. We did devotionals as a family, but not as often because teenagers scatter. They have other activities that sometimes keep them away from home and it is harder to find a time when we are all together. I have keenly felt the weight of this responsibility when my children have been ready to go to college. When my oldest went away to college, fear completely took over. I would send my son long emails reminding him of God's Word, our beliefs, our desire for him to continue to believe in God. One day, when my son was home on break he told me, "Mom, your emails are like the letters of the Apostle Paul." It wasn't a compliment. It was more like a "Mom, you're no fun. What's going on? You're emails are so motivated by fear that I don't enjoy reading them. Can you stop?" As I re-read my emails, I realized he was right. The truth was, I wasn't really enjoying writing them. As I changed my focus and stopped acting out of fear, we both enjoyed our emails again.

Another reason I would become fearful about my responsibility in regards to their faith is because for my kids, the teenage years are the years they process through what they have believed until then. They look for discrepancies in what they've been taught. They analyze the words and instructions of authority figures. They question almost everything they are taught. It is hard as parents not to take offense in their questioning. Unfortunately, our teens usually process out loud. That is, instead of just thinking and wondering about life, they make statements like, "I don't want to read my Bible," or they ask questions like, "How do we know that Christianity is the only way?" Sometimes it's hard not to take their questions and statements personally and feel like they're questioning us. We become fearful that they are leaving the faith or are going to make different decisions than we have taught them, but most teens just want to be able to say they believe something because they've done the hard work of figuring it out for themselves and not simply because that's what their parents believe. In fact, there is an underlying fear in them that if they are not able to defend their beliefs, people will not respect their opinion, and if their beliefs end up being aligned with their parents' beliefs, others will just assume and say, "That's just your parents talking."

When we are driven by fear, we interrupt them when they voice their opinion or ask us questions. We reprimand them for asking questions that we think they should know the answers to. Our fear leads us to speak and behave in ways that are not productive. When our second son went away to college his processing nearly drove me crazy! He began to process ideas and concepts out loud that seemed contrary to what we had taught him. Of course, being the mom, I would think "Where did I go wrong?" Such fear blinds us from the treasure behind what is happening. If we do not interrupt our kids when they speak, if we let them share their doubts and ask us questions, if we put our fear aside, we get to see what is in their hearts. We get an x-ray of their spiritual life. When this happens, we are better able to pray for their specific needs. We discover how we can better help them. Remember that parents are still the most influential people in the lives of our children. We can listen and we can ask questions that will guide them to reason out what they are thinking. If you are strong in your beliefs, then you know that God loves your child more than you do. Parents are simply a vessel through which God can show Himself to them. Be that vessel. Don't just hand them the answers you want them to have. Our faith is not so weak that it cannot withstand a few questions, and they are not going to ask a question that's never been asked. Show confidence in your God by not immediately panicking because they are questioning their faith. Gently guide them to resources. Help them look for answers outside of yourself. Share the story of your own journey to faith; even if you grew up in a Christian home, there had to be a time of questioning. No one should follow Jesus blindly. No one should be a Christian simply because of tradition. Everyone has their own journey. Let them know that their questioning is not abnormal. Keep the dialog open and help them find the tools they need to find their answers.

For Christians, our faith is the most important legacy we can leave our children. The responsibility of instilling that faith can be very scary. Yet, I am constantly reminded and reassured that I am not doing it alone. Our responsibility while they are living at home is to be an example, talk to them about God, give them opportunities to see God in everything, be the best Christians we can be and show them how God is merciful and gracious even when we are not. We will never be able to do all these things perfectly, but asking God for direction and being constantly in a state of pursuing these goals will help us not be so fearful. The connection with God, being proactive about their faith, will make us feel like something is being done instead of feeling guilty because nothing is getting done.

There is another point regarding our children's faith that I would like to bring up because it appears to have no bearing on their faith, but in fact has more to do with their faith than devotionals, praying with them or taking them to church. That is, our relationship with our husbands. I will speak more on the fear that specifically accompanies that relationship, but for now I will share how it affects our children's faith.

As parents we chose to homeschool for different reasons. For some it's because we enjoy spending time with them. We want to protect them from the outside world. We want to be involved in their lives. We want teach them about God. None of these desires are wrong. In fact, we are blessed to be able to spend time with them, protect them from real dangers, and be able to speak into and have an impact on their lives. The danger is that while we are doing these good things, we forget about our spouse. He's the guy that makes it possible for me to stay home and raise these children. After awhile of homeschooling and being busy with extra activities, field trips, sports, etc., we neglect the most important relationship we have outside of our relationship with God. And we think it's justified, because we are doing a noble work. In fact, our husbands also are convinced that it's justified.

The less we work on our marriage, the less we want to. We become used to not being together. We become used to making decisions on our own and just letting our husbands know what's on the calendar, where he needs to be and when. We start to treat him like one of the kids! When our husbands don't feel respected, they often protect themselves by becoming distant. Because we want to be loved, we pursue them. But our pursuit is critical and demanding. Before you know it, the nice Christian homeschool couple are yelling at each other and fighting in front of their nice Christian homeschool kids. Sure, no one outside the family knows, but the people who matter the most do. The relationship between their Christian parents will be one of the greatest contributors in our children's decision to follow Jesus or not.

In the New Testament, when Jesus was advocating for marriage, He was asked by those who wanted to put Him on the spot, why the Old Testament leader Moses had allowed divorce. Jesus answered that it was because of the hardness of their hearts, but that in the beginning, that had not been God's intention. Humans can be stubborn, stubborn, stubborn people. We want what we want, we want it when we want it and we want it how we want it, and we usually think we're justified in our stubborness. This is the hardness of our hearts. In marriage one of our greatest challenges is to be givers instead of takers. It is easier to blame the other person than to admit our own faults. Ironically, even an admittance of guilt would be better for our kids than the constant bickering and defensiveness that goes on in marriages…even homeschool marriages. Don't let that happen to you. Don't let that happen to your kids. One of the best things we can do to help our kids in their journey of faith is to love our husbands and show it.

I have seen the sense of pride my kids have when they know my husband and I love each other. When they see us express that love, they are confident that we not only teach them that God wants them to love and forgive each other. We do not only tell them that God is faithful, but we show them through loving and forgiving each other. They know that it is God who has kept us together. They are assured that putting God's principles into practice is not a waste of time. They are confident that we are the same people at home that we are when we are away from home. If we allow Satan to destroy our marriage, we allow him to destroy much more than we can possibly imagine, and we will regret it. No amount of self-fulfillment, no degree of "freedom," no measure of justification will make up for the realization of having been a stumbling block to our own children. As I write this, I am so passionate about getting this across to you that I cry just thinking of what can be lost. Please, keep your marriage second only to your relationship with God.

Homework for the homeschool mom:

What is your greatest fear about your children's academics? If that happens, what is the worst thing that can come out of that? Is it really bad? Can something good come from it?

Are there changes you need to make in your children's academics that you have been afraid to make? Why?

What are you doing to help your child in his spiritual growth? What are you doing to help your own spiritual growth?

Since our marriage relationship greatly affects our children's faith, how do you and your spouse actively seek keeping your marriage relationship growing? (Ex.: date nights, marriage retreats, weekend outings)

Have you and your spouse fallen into any of the neglectful habits mentioned in this chapter in regards to your marriage? Make a plan and commitment together to bring your marriage up to a level that you consider healthy.

Chapter 8

What if We Ruin Our Kids?

Homeschooling: Do it Afraid
(The Fear of Failure)

What do you picture when you think of the word success? What is most important to you? What is your measuring stick? How do you know when you have accomplished success? I believe that most of society believes that success includes a college education, a high paying job, the most updated gadgets, being married with one or two kids, a big house, expensive vacations, etc, etc. We are constantly measured by this idea and we judge others on that same criteria. However, when I really think about it, that is a very superficial idea of success.

Look at what Jesus says in the parable of the sower, found in the gospel of Mark.

> "Listen! Behold, a sower went out to sow. And it happened, as he sowed, that some seed fell by the wayside; and the birds of the air came and devoured it. Some fell on stony ground, where it did not have much earth; and immediately it sprang up because it had no depth of earth. But when the sun was up it was

scorched, and because it had no root it withered away. And some seed fell among thorns; and the thorns grew up and choked it, and it yielded no crop. But other seed fell on good ground and yielded a crop that sprang up, increased and produced: some thirtyfold, some sixty, and some a hundred" (Mark 4:3-8).

Later, Jesus tells His disciples what the parable means.

"The sower sows the word. And these are the ones by the wayside where the word is sown. When they hear, Satan comes immediately and takes away the word that was sown in their hearts. These likewise are the ones sown on stony ground who, when they hear the word, immediately receive it with gladness; and they have no root in themselves, and so endure only for a time. Afterward, when tribulation or persecution arises for the word's sake, immediately they stumble. Now these are the ones sown among thorns, they are the ones who hear the word, and the cares of this world, the deceitfulness of riches and the desires for other things entering in choke the word, and it becomes unfruitful. But these are the ones sown on good ground, those who hear the word, accept it, and bear fruit: some thirtyfold, some sixty, and some a hundred" (Mark 4:14-20).

What is God's idea of success? To be good ground. Therefore, as parents our greatest task is to prepare our children to be good ground, so that when they hear the word, they will accept it, and bear fruit. "What shall it profit a man, if he shall gain the whole world, and lose his own soul" (Mark 8:36)? As a mom, I often think, what shall it profit me, if I get the perfect curriculum and lose my kids? What shall it profit me if I get them into college and they lose their way? What shall it profit them to find a job they enjoy if they lose their soul?

Many of you would probably concede that this is the highest form of success. Yet I challenge you to do the hard thing that I often have to do. Evaluate where you spend most of your effort. Is God at the center of what we do or is He on the side? Is He intertwined in our lives or is He specifically set aside for Sunday mornings? "For where our treasure is, there our heart will be also" (Luke 12:34). I admit that I have often skipped family devotionals because we were running late for "school." We don't often pray together because everyone is running in different directions. According the Jesus, the cares of this world choke the seed out of our daily lives. Consider this, while our children are living at home, we have the opportunity to prepare the ground. To teach them about God. Isaiah 55:11 tells us the God's Word never comes back to Him empty, "but will accomplish what He desires and achieves the purpose for which He sent it." If we make God a priority in our lives, our children will have a better chance of making Him a priority in their lives. If we put our relationship with God even above society's idea of success, our children will see it, but it must be genuine. It must first be in our hearts. "For out of the abundance of the heart, the mouth speaks" (Luke 6:45). That is our true evaluator. What comes out of our mouth?

What motivation do we give our little ones? What is our own motivation? What are we trying to accomplish? Spoken or unspoken, our motivation comes shining through in the way we express ourselves, in the things we tell our kids, in the way we pick our kids' activities and in the things we say yes and no to. Are we motivated by fear? That comes shining through too, and our fear makes our children insecure. Do we see our children's "success" as a reflection on us? Graduating one of our children can make us feel successful. We feel we have accomplished what we set out to do. That is a good feeling, but we must guard our hearts. Is it our success, or is it a reason to be grateful to God? If we take all the glory, what does that say to our kids about our relationship with God? Do our beliefs lead us to depend on God or to use God for our own purposes?

Our pastor at church has talked many times about the different stages people are in in their spiritual walk. There are people far from God, there are those who have questions about faith and are not yet sure what they believe, there are new Christians, there are growing Christians, and mature Christians. He said that the hardest jump is from growing Christians to mature Christians. Most people spend their whole life in the growing Christians category.

I admire Christians who leave their own agendas to follow God's. Would we let go of our agenda if God suddenly called us to do something completely different? How do we respond when we find out our daughter has a learning disability, or we can't afford a particular class, or our son is completely different from us, or our child wants to study something that will not make him a lot of money. How do we handle it? If our children choose not to go to college, would we trust that God had a plan, or would we pressure and guilt our kids into going to college anyway? How we respond to these many, many, many situations, reveals what is in our hearts. It reveals where our treasure is. It is not pretty sometimes, but take a good look, because once we know where we are, we can make the necessary adjustments.

Redefining Success

I once heard a homeschool mom say some of the most defeated words a mom can say, "All my kids have turned out badly and the only common denominator is me, so I don't have to look too far to see whose fault it is." We were in a crowded room and there was a lot going on so I didn't get to respond, but my heart broke for her and

Homeschooling: Do It Afraid

what she was feeling. If I could sit down for coffee with her, I would tell her three stories.

When I was a teenager, I was one of the most egotistical, self-absorbed, lying-to-get-my-way and covering my tracks experts who never got caught. I had my parents thinking that my teachers didn't like me and my teachers thought my parents didn't care. When I went to college I skipped most of my classes and I was pregnant and married by the age of nineteen. While I did have challenges at home that I could always blame, the truth is, my heart was dark. By the time I was twenty-four, my husband and I were headed for divorce. We had two children at the time.

God was relentless in His pursuit of me. My husband began his faith journey with God and started going to church. His church friends started praying for me. Everywhere I went for the next year, I ran into crazy Christians who wanted to tell me about the love of God. Sometimes I listened, sometimes I didn't, but always, God was determined. Finally, one day when I was listening to Christian radio, the pastor invited listeners to make a commitment to follow Christ. I kneeled by my radio and started a spiritual journey that changed my life and my eternity. No one could have ever guessed it; no one could have predicted it. I was an angry, fearful, hopeless wife and mother who had made a lot of mistakes, and here God was giving me a chance to start over. I am forever grateful for His love, compassion, mercy, and grace. Unlike those who were always moral and "good," I have no problem understanding that I love God because He loved me first. I know about mercy and grace because I know who I was and where He took me out of. I know He did it because of His own goodness, not mine. Whenever someone comes up to me and tells me about some family member who "will never change," I cringe. From my own experience, I learned that nothing is impossible for God. Not even me.

Silvia Escobar

The second story is that of a couple I met about twenty years ago. The wife had been coming to church for a couple of years, but her husband was not receptive to the things of God. One day, she pulled me aside and said, "I'm done. There have been so many things going on, it's ridiculous. Today when I get home, I am leaving him. I wanted to thank you for all your help, but it's no use. He will never change." Without even thinking, I started to tell her that no one ever knows what God is doing in the background. God is always working. You cannot be sure that nothing is happening because you cannot see your husband's heart. Imagine your husband is walking through a long, dark tunnel. He has been in darkness all his life, but God is getting ready to show him the exit and Satan senses it. He starts to put obstacles in his path. He tries to sabotage God's work, to stop your husband from taking a turn that might lead to the light at the end of the tunnel. But he cannot stop it. I believe it will come. If you give up now, you're going to miss it." To this day, I do not believe that came from me. That night, at a Bible study her husband decided to attend with her, he became a Christian-seemingly from nowhere, and totally unexpected. They became a blessing to the church we attended for many years before they moved away to serve elsewhere. From this story I learned that God is always working. Even when we can't see it with our own eyes, we need to trust that He does not slumber nor sleep (Psalm 121).

The third and last story is sad, and yet also comforting. One of my college professors shared that all through his teenage years and most of his adult life, he was on drugs, drunk, losing jobs, and getting divorced and remarried. Later in his adult life, he came to faith in Christ and his life changed. He went back to school and got his Masters in Psychology and Theology. Out of all the mistakes he made and all the things he regrets, the one he mentioned the most was that his mother did not live long enough to see him come to Christ. She had raised him in a Christian home and had prayed for him all his life. She witnessed most of his destructive behavior, but never got to see the redemption.

In some ways, this is a sad story, but it reminds me that we are only contributors in our children's lives. God's plan is bigger than us. It is higher than our plans. I used to think I needed to be present and connected to every important or spiritual milestone my kids reached. While that would be nice, I don't need to anymore. I know that the most important thing is for them to have a personal relationship with Jesus, to repent of their sins and to understand that God has saved them from their sins through faith and not by anything they could do. I want them to grow in their relationship with God, to love Him and to love people. I am a steward of their lives while they are home, but their lives belong to God. He loves them more than I do. At times that is hard for me to believe, because I love them so much, but it comforts me to know that long after they have left my home, God will still be working. This is His plan, not mine. I am part of His plan, He is not part of mine. That has become a great comfort to me.

I know that we cannot guarantee that all our children will be saved. They need to choose to follow Christ, we cannot do it for them. I know that we are not perfect and that it is easy to beat ourselves up and blame ourselves for the way they turn out. And yes, some of it will most definitely be our fault, but the truth is, whether it is easy to see our faults and our children's faults because our kids are making many mistakes, or whether we are unaware of it because our kids are just so perfect, EVERY good thing comes from God (James 1:17). "From everyone who has been given much, much will be demanded; and from the one who has been entrusted with much, much more will be asked" (Luke 12:48). "And all things work together for good to those who love the Lord and are called to His purpose" (Romans 8:28). There is no getting around it. We do not have the power to produce perfect children, nor do we have the power to mess them up beyond repair. We just don't. So let's stop thinking of ourselves more highly than we ought to and thank the Lord for the privilege of raising our children and let's stop beating ourselves up if our kids are going down the wrong path. The Lord is not finished yet! Success and failure are best left to be determined by the One who set the standard in the first place.

Homework for the homeschool mom:

What do you see today in your child that makes you fearful for the future? What can you do to change it? What can you not do?

How do you react to those fears? Do you beat yourself up? If you know for a fact that you are directly responsible, ask God to forgive you. And then ask Him to help you forgive yourself.

Speak truth to yourself in regard to your child. God's word is true. Here are a few verses to get you started.

> "The Lord is my shepherd, I shall not want" (Psalm 23:1).
>
> "He tends his flock like a shepherd: He gathers the lambs in his arms and carries them close to his heart; he gently leads those that have young" (Isaiah 40:11).
>
> "So we do not lose heart. Though our outer self is wasting away, our inner self is being renewed day by day. For this light momentary affliction is preparing for us an eternal weight of glory beyond all comparison, as we look not to the things that are seen, but to the things that are unseen. For the things that are seen are transient, but the things that are unseen are eternal" (2 Corinthians 4:16-18).
>
> "Now faith is the assurance of things hoped for, the conviction of things not seen" (Hebrews 11:1).

Chapter 9

What Will I Do When the Kids Leave?

Homeschooling: Do it with the End in Mind
(Fear of the Future)

The summer before my oldest son Alex went away to college, I cried and cried and cried. It wasn't just because I was going to miss him, although that was a big part of it; life, as I had known it for the last nine years, was over. Taking vacations in October, family nights with everyone home, dinner with all of us sitting at the table, field trips with all six of my children…over. This was the end of an era. I knew it and I was overwhelmed with grief at the impending loss. He was leaving and he was anxious to go. Anytime anyone asked him what his plans were, he would talk about the college he was going to and how far away it was. They would ask, "Are you ready?," and he would answer, "Are you kidding? I have a U-haul rented and ready to go!" That answer used to make me so angry. It was like he was so miserable here that he couldn't wait to leave. A month before he left, we threw him a party to celebrate his achievement and to give everyone an opportunity to wish him well and say goodbye. Of course, in one of his conversations with a group of friends, he gave the same answer. "I can't wait. I have a U-haul rented and ready to go." I said, "I don't know why you need a U-haul, you don't OWN anything!" Well, everyone thought that was funny, but I knew I was angry. I didn't like what I was feeling: fear.

As I have said before, fear is a horrible master. It makes us say and do things that we don't want to say and do. In my case, it was stopping me from enjoying this milestone with my son. Instead, I was afraid of the changes that lay ahead and the reality that this was the beginning of the end. People always say change is good. But usually it is said to comfort someone who is in the middle of a change they didn't want. That is where I was. I did not know what my family would look like without my oldest at home and I did not know how our relationship with our oldest would change. NOTHING would ever be the same. The dynamics were about to change and I didn't have a choice. The day when we took our son to college with all his stuff (didn't need a u-haul after all), I soaked it all in. We went with him to finish his paperwork and look over his classes. We went to orientation and made the tuition payment. The next day was the big day, moving him in, meeting his roommate, and working our way to the end of the day when we would say good-bye. I was fine all the way through until we hugged and I looked in his eyes. I told him he'd be fine, I told him we'd see him in a couple of months, we all got in a circle and prayed, we got in the van, and I cried all the way home… and I prayed like mad.

Five years later, I went through the same thing with our second son, Miguel. Even though he was older and I felt he was more prepared because of that, the same fears resurfaced. I felt like I was saying good-bye all summer. Then we went through orientation together, met his roommate and came to the end of the day when we said good-bye. We hugged, I looked in his eyes and told him he'd be fine, we'd see him in a couple of months. We got in a circle and prayed, we got in the van, and I cried all the way home…and I prayed like mad.

Alex has been married for years now. So far I have two granddaughters. My second, Miguel, lives in Seattle and is in graduate school. He went from saying all through homeschooling, "College is not for me," to "Everyone should go to college just for the experience." My third son Isaac is finishing up at Columbia College in Chicago My fourth, Christy, is at Trinity International University, and as I finish my last run through this book, my fifth, David, is starting at Indiana Wesleyan University and Kathy is the only one at home now.

The fear that I had, the fear of change in the future, did come to pass. Just as I suspected, everything changed and everything has continued to change. Nothing is the same…it's different. But different isn't necessarily bad. Every season in our family has been special. The season when my children were all at home is a special memory. The season when my second oldest became the oldest and deepened his relationship with his siblings is also very special. Having the last four at home and watching them do things together because they are closer in age, also special. And so it has continued. Always changing, always different. I am learning that change is good. It is necessary. All healthy, living organisms change and grow. My family is a living organism. Change is a sign of health, so I am thankful for the change. The key for me, is to be present at every stage. To savor it, enjoy it, learn from it, because when it's over, it's over. Something new will come to take it's place and then I will get to enjoy that too!

In 2014 I had a scare that I want to share with you. We were at a training for marriage conference speakers. We were in Miami, but we were busy training. We were in sessions from 8:00 am to 9:30 pm all week. It ended the day before Easter Sunday and we planned to get home early Sunday morning in time to have Easter dinner with our family. They had been eagerly waiting, dicing and cleaning. Easter morning we had to be up at 3 am. As I got out of bed, I didn't feel well. I felt a heaviness in my chest and a pain coming up my left arm. This made me feel anxious, so I didn't know if I was feeling nauseous from the pain or from the anxiety. As I finished packing, I prayed that I would start to feel better, but the pain and the anxiety did not subside. As we arrived at the airport, I felt something was very wrong. I kept having to go to the restroom—making it difficult to check in at the airline. It was clear that I was not going to be able to get on the plane. An ambulance was called and I was taken to the emergency room where they determined that I did not have a heart attack but needed to be observed for 24 hours.

This was the first time I actually considered the very real possibility of dying and never seeing my kids again. It was very overwhelming. I was anxious at the thought of not seeing them, but my anxiety increased much more at the thought of them not being able to have their mom. The questions that immediately came to my mind, there as I sat in the airport, was, "Are they ready? Are they ready to make it on their own? Will they be fine without me?" When we talked later, as I lay in the hospital, I encouraged them to continue with the plans and to celebrate Easter without us. One of my sons had even invited some friends of ours to go to church with them. My brother and sister-in-law were bringing the turkey and my kids would put everything else together. Sitting in the hospital, I texted my kids and asked them to send pictures of what was going on at home. They did. Sure, they missed us, but they were doing a great job.

My children still need me for certain things and I know my job is not done, but it does my heart good to know that if the Lord were to call me home sooner rather than later, they would be fine. They know how to take care of themselves and each other. In our case that is largely due to our faith and our homeschooling. I may not know what the future holds, but I am certain that God will continue to strengthen us and prepare us for the task ahead.

That same year a family we knew experienced a tragic loss. The dad and two of their children went camping. In the middle of the night, a tree fell on their tent and killed their ten year old daughter, the youngest in the family. I cannot imagine the pain and anguish that this family experienced and the loss they will most certainly always feel. They will never be the same again. I heard the dad being interviewed on the news talk about the sovereignty of God and I was amazed. How can a parent speak of the sovereignty of God in the midst of such a loss? I can only assume that the promises of God are true. That God gives us strength to endure the tragedies, the losses and the disappointments in our lives. That He uses these things for good to mold us to be more like Christ. That He loves us and desires good, not evil. These are the promises all believers hold on to. In this life, we will have trouble, but we take courage in the knowledge that Jesus has overcome the world. That His comfort and peace can be beyond understanding. This is our hope.

There is something else that came to mind after hearing this news. I thanked God they had been homeschooling. I would say that this tragedy cut that family's time prematurely, but the truth is, none of us knows how much time we have, nor how much time our children will be with us. What a gift to be able to spend so much time with our children now. "Be very careful, then, how you live--not as unwise but as wise, making the most of every opportunity, because the days are evil" (Ephesians 5:15,16). What a blessing to be able to have our children close to us for as long as we homeschool. This is the time to make the most of relationships. This is the time to laugh and not take ourselves too seriously. This is the time to enjoy the family that God has given us with all its cracks and imperfections. This is the time to be present. It is so easy to worry, to be fearful, to be hesitant, to be uncertain, but why do we worry about things we cannot control? Make the best of the moments you have, for tomorrow will have its own troubles.

Finding Fulfillment in a New Season

Here is another thing I have feared about the future—post homeschooling. It's kind of cruel to bring me home from the workforce kicking and screaming, only to find that I loved being home, only to realize that it's temporary. The question that I have found myself asking is, "What will I do when all my kids are done?" I've invested my whole life in this. Now what? In my case, because of our financial challenges, I know that I will have to go to work. The time will be here sooner rather than later. When my kids were all little, people would say as they passed me by, "Enjoy them now. It goes by quickly." Don't you hate when someone tells you that while you're trying to figure out how to homeschool while nursing and trying to stay awake? But guess what…it does.

Because time goes so quickly, I would suggest you not shelf your gifts, talents and hobbies while you're raising and homeschooling your kids. It's easy for us to just say, "I guess this will have to wait until I finish raising my kids." Instead, use those gifts and talents in the process of raising your family. Let's say you love to write. How can you implement that in your homeschooling? Teaching it, of course, but how about journaling? Or leaving notes for your children? How about a Facebook page or blog? Incorporate what you like to do into your daily life, even if it's just for a little while. Show your children you are a real person with real interests and abilities. It will bless them to know it, especially your daughters. As your children get older, find a place to volunteer where you can use your gifts. On days when motherhood and homeschooling are all consuming, continuing to be who God created you to be will help you remember that you are so much more than just "mom." You are a child of God with your own gifts, talents and strengths. The more our identity is dependent on our role, the more difficult it will be when it changes or when it is over. In contrast, the more aware of who we are and what we can do well, the easier it will be to look forward to the possibilities that exist in a new season with more time and freedom.

Throughout most of my homeschooling years I have volunteered at our church in several roles. I have been a Sunday School teacher, a Vacation Bible School organizer, an adult Bible study teacher, a small group leader, and a workshop speaker. These have not all happened at once, and there have been other serving opportunities that I have had to say no to, but through the years, one thing has been constant in my volunteer work: teaching. I love to teach. Actually, I like to teach and empower.

Several years ago, God impressed on me the need to start thinking about my post homeschool days. It happened shortly after my mother passed away. Meditating on her life and wondering what my life would look like at the end, brought me to ask some rather hard questions. One of the things that changed when my mom passed away, was that I started to spend more time with my dad. My dad liked simple things. One of them was eating at buffets. So, when I visited him we would go to lunch at one. I noticed all the elderly people, not eating, but working there. My dad talked with the servers and found out that they were working there because they had to. They just didn't have enough to retire on. Then I started noticing this at other places too. I started to get an unsettling feeling that in a few years, it could be me. Working at a place I don't want to work at because I had to. I do believe that honest work is a good thing and you do what you have to do when you have to do it, but if you don't want to do it, you better make plans to do something else. That's when I started to take inventory of my life and where I wanted it to go.

All through my volunteer work, my goal has been to empower people to be the person God intended them to be by giving them the tools they need and showing them how much God is for them. I also want to be available when my kids call me to ask if I can babysit my grandkids. I want to have Thanksgiving at my house and be there for holidays. I want to be able to just get up and go. But I'm going to need to make a living.

So my question became, "When I am finished homeschooling, how can I make a living doing what I love and have the flexibility to be there for my family?" The last thing on my mind was to go back to school and finish my degree in Psychology, but that is exactly what came to mind. I thought that was just in my head. After all, we were losing our house, I was taking care of my dad and I was still homeschooling! So I took baby steps. Each time I took one, I thought, "For sure the whole thing will fall apart here." I started by doing some research on the different Christian colleges with adult programs. I applied to one where most of the work was reading and writing and they met once a week. I submitted my college transcripts and was accepted. I filled out scholarship applications and discovered my tuition would all be covered with scholarships. I started school and continued homeschooling.

I was able to finish a few years ago. When I graduated I was reminded of two valuable lessons. First, to finish something, you have to start. Second, time passes whether you start or not. I am currently a Woman and Family Coach. I teach parenting classes at churches, organizations and public schools. All the while, my priority is my family. Making plans for the future has taken some of the fear out of change. When I finish homeschooling, this season of my life will end and another will begin. That's not a bad thing, it's just different.

A Marriage That Lasts a Lifetime.

For some couples, the day they say goodbye to the last child leaving home will be one of the scariest days of their lives. They will look at each other and wonder how their marriage will survive not having the children keeping them busy and distracted from the fact that they never really got along or did not deal with the issues that have strained their relationship.

Working on our marriage throughout our homeschooling years is key to having a fulfilling marriage after our nest is empty. It is necessary to make plans for those years. Talking about those plans, working toward them together can help us keep an eye toward the future. It might even help us to keep balance in the present. The idea of retiring is seeming less and less attractive to me as I get older. Retiring from what? There is so much work to do in the world and we have an opportunity to make a difference our whole lives. Part of that opportunity is through our marriage. People long to see a marriage that is truly committed "'till death do us part." Somewhere around mid-life, in their forties and fifties, couples start to get itchy. They start looking back and wanting to know that they have made good choices. That they have spent their life well so far. They are keenly aware that they probably have less time left in front of them than what they've left behind. They want to know that they are going in the right direction. If their marriage is a little shaky, they may do things they regret. But when they look at you, a Christian couple who have withstood the test of time, who have raised their children the best they could, who are honest about their ups and downs, their strengths and weaknesses, their good choices as well as their mistakes, and how God has gotten them through it all, they will be reminded that God does not lie. His promises are true. He is finishing the work He has started in you. If that couple, full of fears and doubts, does not give up. if they do not give in to fear, they too will have a marriage that lasts a lifetime. (Remember: that couple may be some random couple at church, but it could also be your son or daughter with their spouse.) "Therefore do not worry about tomorrow, for tomorrow will worry about itself. Each day has enough trouble of its own." (Matthew 6:34)

Silvia Escobar

Homework for the homeschool mom:

As God reveals to you the possibilities of what He can do in and through your family, write them down.

What kind of legacy do you want to leave your children? How can you, with God's help, accomplish this?

Talk to your husband about the empty nest days. What do you see yourselves doing together in that season? What things do you have to do today in order to prepare for that outcome?

Conclusion

I've worked on this book for a few years, but the lessons have come over a lifetime and continue to do so. And so it will be with you. Some of my experiences might have resonated with your own, some might be foreign to you, but one thing is for sure, your family will make its own story. Even in similarities with other homeschool families, your perception, your different responses, the choices you make and God's call on your family will make your experience unique. We may not always know what God will do with that child who still can't spell correctly in Senior year, or the one who wants to be a musician and you wonder how she's going to pay her bills, or the one who has said hurtful words to you and you wonder how he will ever fit into society. A mother's fears can go on and on, but remember that our hope was never in our own success or even in our child's abilities. Our hope is in God. In my own times of trouble and challenge, the words that God has spoken to my heart over and over again are: "I will impress you again." And He has…over and over again. So I do it afraid. I do not wait for the fear to leave, because whether or not I'm afraid is not relevant. It only matters that God is in control. It only matters that He has been faithful and that He is the same yesterday, today and always. "Things which eye has not seen and ear has not heard, and which have not entered the heart of man, all that God has prepared for those who love Him" (1 Corinthians 2:9,10). And so it will be with you.